BRAHMANI SWAYAMPAAK

Culinary Secrets from a Deshastha Brahmin Kitchen

Vasudha Gawande

Translation by

Ketki M. V. Gawande

Popular Prakashan

www.popularprakashan.com

Published by
Asmita Mohite for
POPULAR PRAKASHAN PVT. LTD.
301, Mahalaxmi Chambers
22, Bhulabhai Desai Road
Mumbai - 400 026
info@popularprakashan.com

First Published 2023

(4549)
ISBN: 978-81-948714-1-5

Cover Design & Inside Layout: Gopi Kukde
Cover Photography: Mangesh Parab
Typesetting: Anjali Sawant

PRINTED IN INDIA
by Repro India Ltd.
Lower Parel,
Mumbai 400013

I dedicate this book
to my husband,
Ratnakar Krishnaji Gawande,
who was my inspiration.

Contents

Foreword

This compilation and treasure of authentic, simple and tasty recipes was done by my mumma, Madhuri Gawande, as a mark of gratitude and respect towards my aaji, Vasudha Gawande, from whom she learnt all of them. As my mother discovered, these amazing recipes were not only easy to make, but were also very nutritious, yummy and healthy.

The original Marathi book, *Brahmani Swayampaak* was thus conceptualised, and is still available everywhere. The book received a fantastic response from everyone, along with several requests from people to translate it into English, so that no one was deprived of this amazing book and cuisine. So, I decided to translate the book into English, and the result is in your hands.

I have always wanted to share my aaji's recipes with the world, and I hope you enjoy them, as much as I did growing up. Thank you for your love and appreciation for my efforts, as well as for this unique cuisine.

— Ketki M. V. Gawande
10th May 2019

Foreword

Born and raised in a typical Deshastha Brahmin family, I learnt all my culinary skills from my mother and the other older women of the community. From my childhood, it was prevalent, that cooking was the essential skill all girls needed to expertise in. As I grew older, I picked up the nuances from all those around me, and my keen observation and passion for food helped me get better in the kitchen. After my marriage, my husband's love for good food became my motivation to learn more and more. He proved to be my guru, as well as my critic.

When my daughter-in-law, Madhuri decided to compile my recipes on my 71st birthday, I was simply overwhelmed. I had never thought that I would be the author of a cook book. My son, Vinayak undertook this mission, and the result was the first Marathi edition, which is widely available today. After its success, my granddaughter, Ketki decided to translate it into English, as she wanted my recipes to be available to all. The result is the book you are reading right now.

Gopi Kukde is the creative brain behind this attractive book. Sanjeev Kapoor, the master chef of India, has kindly put in a foreword for me. Sanjeev has always enjoyed my recipes and I have enjoyed cooking for him. Harsha Bhatkal, my publisher and a son to me, has continuously inspired me to add more and more recipes to this book. I thank them all for their time and generosity.

Throughout my life, it's been my family that continuously drives my passion for food and cooking, and I'm very grateful for their support. My entire family and all my extended family are my backbone and I feel extremely happy that they love my food. For a mother and a grandmother nothing can be more satisfying than to see her children enjoying her recipes and proudly sharing them.

— Vasudha R. Gawande

Preface

Many years ago, we had all gathered at my friend's Madhuri and Vinayak's home, to celebrate the success of my first book. It was a simple homely affair, and Vinayak's mother had cooked a meal for all of us. That is when I fell in love with the simple, easy to make, yet so delicious Brahmani cuisine.

What fascinated me was the way a Brahmin taat (thali) was presented, with a left side and right side. On the left are the salt, pickles, chatnis and koshimbir and on the right is the bhaaji, usal and aamti dahi. In the centre is the poli, a small portion of bhaat and the pakwaane. The entire taat looks like a beautiful rangoli of dishes of various colours and flavours, tempting all the senses to soulfully enjoy them.

This is not just food, but it is a culture we should be extremely proud of, and it's crucial that this heritage gets propagated forward and inherited by future generations. The specialty of this cuisine is that it's healthy, nutritious and utterly yummy recipes can be made with simple ingredients and minimal efforts. This is comfort food which satisfies your body, mind and soul, as it's made in your home by your loved ones for you. So please enjoy these recipes with lot of love as that is most important ingredient here.

— Sanjeev Kapoor
10th May 2019

Masala

The main tastemakers, masalas are the spices used in the recipes and play a very integral role. In Brahmani cuisine, the favourites are red chilli powder, turmeric powder, coriander-cumin powder, and godaa or kaala masala, which is the speciality of the Brahmins. These masalas enhance the aroma and flavour of your dishes. All these masalas can easily be prepared fresh at home and are also readily available in the market.

Godaa Masala

- ¼ kg green coriander seeds
- 100 grams cumin seeds
- 50 grams black cumin seeds (shah jeera)
- 50 grams star anise (chakri phool)
- 50 grams cinnamon
- 50 grams cloves
- 50 grams peppercorns
- 50 grams lichen (dagdaphool)
- 50 grams cobra saffron (nagkesar)
- 5-6 bay leaves (tamaal patra)
- 4-5 black cardamoms (kali velchi)
- 1 nutmeg (jaiphal)
- 50 grams Sankeshwari chillies
- 25 grams poppy seeds
- 50 grams black sesame seeds (kale til)
- 50 grams white sesame seeds (safed til)
- 2 tablespoons oil
- 2 teaspoons turmeric powder
- 1 vati dried coconut, chopped into thin slices
- 2 teaspoons salt

- Clean and dry all the dry ingredients.
- Heat a pan or kadai, dry-roast the black and white sesame seeds without oil and set aside.
- Heat the oil in a pan on low heat. Add all the dry ingredients and lastly add the sesame seeds. Slow roast on low heat for about 10-15 minutes and till the aroma sets in. Do not roast on high heat as the spices will get burnt.
- Cool and grind to a powder. Store in a tight lid jar.

Dhana-Jeera Masala

¼ kg coriander seeds (dhane)

50 grams cumin seeds (jeera)

1 inch cinnamon

2-3 cloves

2-3 peppercorns

Clean and dry all the ingredients.

Heat a pan or kadai and dry-roast the ingredients on low heat till fragrant. Do not roast on high heat as the spices will get burnt.

Cool and grind to a powder. Store in a tight lid jar.

Sambar Masala

1 vati split Bengal gram (chana dal)

½ vati coriander seeds

¼ vati skinless split black gram (udid dal)

1 teaspoon fenugreek seeds (methi seeds)

10-12 dried red chillies

2 teaspoons cumin seeds

15-20 curry leaves

1 teaspoon rice

4-5 peppercorns

1 teaspoon asafoetida (hing)

¼ teaspoon turmeric powder

Heat a pan or kadai and dry-roast all the ingredients on low heat, except the asafoetida and turmeric powder.

Allow them to cool and then add the asafoetida and turmeric powder.

Grind to a powder. Store in a tight lid jar.

Vaalvan

These are dry snacks, that are prepared in advance and saved for a rainy day.

Tandul Phenyaa

- 1 vati rice (tandul)
- 5 vatis water
- 1 teaspoon poppy seeds (khas khas)
- 1 teaspoon asafoetida
- Salt to taste

Soak the rice in water overnight. Strain the water the next day and re-soak the rice in fresh water.

The next day, strain the water again and re-soak the rice in fresh water.

After three days, strain the water from the rice using a colander. Spread the rice on a clean cloth, to dry in the sun.

Once dried, add 5 vatis of water, poppy seeds, asafoetida and salt to the rice. This will result in a runny mixture.

Spread a clean cloth and pour ladlefuls of the mixture at a distance of 2-3 inches on the cloth, and allow it to dry, preferably in sunlight.

Store in a tight lid jar.

Sabudanya Chikvadyaa

- 1 vati sago (sabudana), soaked overnight
- 1 teaspoon cumin seeds
- Salt to taste
- 2½ vatis water

Place a pan on low heat and add the soaked sago, cumin seeds and salt.

Add the water and cook on low heat till the sago becomes transparent.

Spread a plastic sheet and pour ladlefuls of the mixture at a distance of 2-3 inches on a clean cloth and allow it to dry, preferably in sunlight.

Store in a tight lid jar.

Sandge

- 1 vati skinless split black gram (udid dal), soaked overnight
- ½ vati skinless split green gram (moong dal), soaked overnight
- 1 inch ginger
- 3-4 green chillies
- 1 teaspoon cumin seeds
- Salt to taste

- Grind together the black gram, green gram, ginger, green chillies, cumin seeds and salt.
- Spread a plastic sheet and pour a tablespoon of the mixture at a distance of 2-3 inches and allow it to dry, preferably in sunlight.
- Store in a tight lid jar.

Tip: *Sandge can be used in amatis and bhaajis.*

Batata Kees

- 5 kgs potatoes (batata)

- Parboil the potatoes with a little salt and refrigerate.
- The next day, peel and grate the potatoes in a plate or muslin cloth and allow it to dry by itself. Do not place it in sunlight as it will turn black.
- Store in a tight lid jar.

Tip: *This kees can be used to make chivdas or can be deep-fried and seasoned with chilli powder and salt. It can be added to poha chivdas too.*

Dahi Mirchi

½ kg green dhaboo mirchi
½ kg sour yoghurt (dahi)
1 teaspoon turmeric powder
1 teaspoon asafoetida
2 teaspoons cumin powder
Salt to taste

Tip: *Dhaboo mirchi is a type of green chilli which is short and bulky. It is also called Bhavnagari chilli.*

Slit the chillies lengthways but leave the tops intact so that the chillies can hold the stuffing.

In a bowl, mix together the yoghurt, turmeric powder, asafoetida, cumin powder and salt, to make a marinade.

Place the chillies in the same bowl and stuff them with the marinade.

Allow the chillies to marinate for 2-3 hours, and place them in a plate. Place the plate in sunlight to dry. Preserve the yoghurt mixture in the bowl.

In the evening, place the dried chillies back in the yoghurt mixture to marinate. Continue this till the yoghurt mixture is over and then dry the chillies completely in sunlight again. Once dried, they turn brown and crispy.

Store in a tight lid jar.

Bhaajnya and Peeth

These are accompaniments which can be used as breakfast recipes, as well as accompaniments to any meal.

Daangar

1 vati split Bengal gram (chana dal)

1 vati skinless split black gram (udid dal)

2 teaspoons cumin seeds

Slow-roast the split Bengal gram and skinless split black gram separately, with 1 teaspoon cumin seeds each.

Cool and store in a tight lid jar.

Methkoot

1 vati split Bengal gram (chana dal)

2 teaspoons rice (tandul)

2 teaspoons wheat grains (gehu)

2 teaspoons skinless split black gram (udid dal)

2 teaspoons black peas

1 inch dried ginger

1 inch turmeric piece

¼ inch asafoetida piece

½ teaspoon cumin seeds

½ teaspoon mustard seeds

½ teaspoon fenugreek seeds (methi seeds)

Heat a kadai and dry-roast all the ingredients.

Cool and grind to a coarse powder.

Store in a tight lid jar.

Upvaas Bhaajni

- ½ kg sago (sabudana)
- ½ kg samo seeds (vari tandul)
- ½ kg amaranth grains (rajgirha grains)
- 50 grams cumin seeds

- Heat a kadai and slow roast the sago, after it turns whiter add the rest of the ingredients and slow roast.
- Cool and grind to a coarse flour.
- Store in a tight lid jar.

Thalipeeth Bhaajni

- ½ kg rice (tandul)
- 1 vati skinless split black gram (udid dal)
- 1 vati skinless split green gram (moong dal)
- 1 vati split Bengal gram (chana dal)
- 1 vati sorghum (jowar)
- 1 vati pearl millet (bajri)
- 1 vati wheat grains (gehu)
- ½ vati cumin seeds

- Slow-roast each ingredient separately, on low heat. Cool and grind together to a coarse flour.
- Store in a tight lid jar.

Chakli Bhaajni

- ½ kg unpolished rice
- ¼ kg skinless split black gram (udid dal)
- ¼ kg split Bengal gram (chana dal)
- 50 grams cumin seeds

- Dry-roast each ingredient separately, on low heat. Cool and grind together to a coarse flour.
- Store in a tight lid jar.

Adai Peeth

- ½ kg rice (tandul)
- 200 grams split Bengal gram (chana dal)
- 200 grams skinless split green gram (moong dal)
- 200 grams split red lentils (masoor dal)
- 200 grams skinless split black gram (udid dal)
- 10 grams cumin seeds
- 10 grams fenugreek seeds (methi seeds)

Dry-roast all the ingredients on low heat for 10 minutes. Cool and grind to a coarse flour.

Store in a tight lid jar.

Dhokla Peeth

- 1 vati rice (tandul)
- ½ vati split Bengal gram (chana dal)
- ¼ vati skinless split black gram (udid dal)

Grind all the ingredients to a flour.

Store in a tight lid jar.

Safed Dhokla Peeth

- 1 vati rice (tandul)
- 1 vati skinless split black gram (udid dal)
- 1 teaspoon fenugreek seeds (methi seeds)
- 1 teaspoon oil
- ½ teaspoon salt

Grind all the ingredients to a flour.

Store in a tight lid jar.

Pickles

The tongue tickles when we say pickles! These play a prominent accessory to all meals and snacks. Be prepared to excite your taste buds as pickles can be sweet, sour, spicy and tangy. Every household has their own recipe for different types of pickles (lonchi), which have been inherited from generation to generation. I've shared some of the many chatpata recipes, for your enjoyment!

Limbache Goad Loncha Variation 1

12 limes (limbu)

1 inch ginger

¼ vati salt

3 vatis sugar (saakhar)

2 teaspoons red chilli powder

Cut the limes and ginger into medium sized pieces. Deseed the limes as the seeds will turn the mixture bitter.

Add the salt to the limes and transfer them to a tight lid glass jar or bottle and store it in a dry place for 5-6 days. Shake the bottle once every day.

Then open the jar and add the sugar and red chilli powder and store again for 5-6 days.

The pickle will be ready in about 10-12 days.

Tip: *Adding red chilli powder is optional. Sugar can be substituted with jaggery too.*

Limbache Goad Loncha Variation 2

- 12 limes (limbu)
- 1 inch ginger
- ¼ vati salt
- 1 teaspoon black peppercorns
- 3 vatis sugar (saakhar)
- 2 teaspoons red chilli powder
- 1 lime-sized jaggery ball

- Cut the limes into small pieces. Deseed the limes as the seeds will turn the mixture bitter.
- Clean the ginger and cut it finely or shred it.
- Place the lime pieces, salt, ginger and peppercorns in a tight lid glass jar or bottle for 8 days and shake the bottle once a day.
- After 8 days put the mixture in a mixer and add the sugar, red chilli powder. Remove it and then add the jaggery ball to it. Mix it well. Store it in a tight lid jar.

Limbache Thikhat Loncha Variation 3

- 12 limes (limbu)
- ¾ vati salt
- 1 packet of ready-made loncha masala
- ½ vati oil

- Wash and dry the limes. Add the salt to it and store in an airtight jar or bottle for 2-3 days and mix it once a day.
- Then add the ready-made masala and mix it well. Allow to rest for a day.
- The next day heat the oil, allow it to cool and come to room temperature and then add it to the pickle.
- Mix it well and store in a tight lid jar.

Kairicha Loncha

- ½ kg raw mangoes (kairi)
- 1 vati salt
- ¾ vati mustard seeds
- ½ vati red chilli powder
- ½ teaspoon fenugreek seeds (methi seeds)
- 1 vati water, boiled and cooled
- ½ lemon-sized jaggery ball

For the tempering

- 2 teaspoons oil
- ½ teaspoon mustard seeds and asafoetida together

Wash the mangoes and dry them.

Add the salt and allow it to stay for a day in a covered vessel.

The next day, in a mixer add mustard seeds, red chilli powder, fenugreek seeds and water, and prepare a mixture.

Add the mixture to the mangoes. Allow it to stay for another day.

On the third day, heat the oil and temper it with mustard seeds and asafoetida.

Allow it to cool and then add this oil to the pickle. Add the jaggery as well.

Mix well and store it in a tight lid jar.

No-Oil Kairi Loncha

- ¼ kg raw mangoes (kairi)
- ¾ vati salt
- 100 grams Sankeshwari or Kashmiri red chillies
- ¾ vati mustard seeds
- ¼ teaspoon fenugreek seed powder (methi powder)
- 2 vatis water, boiled and cooled
- ¾ teaspoon asafoetida

Tips:

- *Fenugreek seed powder can be prepared by grinding fenugreek seeds in a mixer.*
- *This pickle has a short shelf life, so make it and enjoy it quickly.*

- Wash and dry the raw mangoes and cut them into small pieces.
- Add the salt to them and allow it to stay for a day in a covered vessel.
- The next day, grind the chillies, mustard seeds, fenugreek seed powder, and water together, and add it to the raw mangoes. Add the asafoetida to it.
- Mix well and store in a tight lid jar.

Kairi Masala Loncha

- ½ kg raw mangoes (kairi)
- ¾ vati salt
- 1 packet of ready-made loncha masala

For the tempering

- 1 lemon-sized jaggery ball
- ½ vati oil
- ½ teaspoon mustard seeds
- ½ teaspoon asafoetida

- Wash and dry the raw mangoes and cut them into small pieces. Add the salt to them and allow it to stay for a day in a covered vessel.
- The next day, add the ready-made masala, mix well and keep it for another day.
- The next day, heat the oil and temper it with mustard seeds and asafoetida. Allow it to cool and add it to the pickle mixture. Store it in a tight lid jar.

Kisslele Kairi Loncha

- 1 vati shredded raw mango (kairi)
- ¼ vati red chilli powder
- ½ vati jaggery
- Salt to taste
- 1 teaspoon cumin seeds

For the tempering

- 2-3 teaspoons oil
- ¼ teaspoon mustard seeds
- ¼ teaspoon asafoetida

Mix all the ingredients together, except for the oil, mustard seeds and asafoetida, and set aside for 5-6 hours.

After that heat the oil and temper it with mustard seeds and asafoetida. Allow it to cool and add it to the mixture.

Mix it well and consume the pickle immediately.

Tip: *This pickle has a short shelf life, so make it and enjoy it quickly.*

Kairicha Chunda

- 1 vati shredded raw Totapuri mango (kairi)
- 1 vati sugar
- ½ vati salt
- 2-3 teaspoons red chilli powder
- 2 teaspoons black peppercorns, crushed
- 2 teaspoons cumin seeds, crushed

Mix all the ingredients and cook on a low heat till it boils and then cool the mixture.

Store it in a tight lid jar.

Kairicha Methamba

- ¼ kg raw mangoes (kairi)
- ¾ vati water
- ¼ kg jaggery
- Red chilli powder, as required
- ½ teaspoon salt

For the tempering

- 2-3 teaspoons oil
- ½ teaspoon mustard seeds
- 1 teaspoon fenugreek seeds (methi seeds)
- ½ teaspoon asafoetida
- ½ teaspoon cumin seeds
- 8-10 curry leaves
- 4-5 red chillies
- ½ teaspoon turmeric powder

- Wash, dry and peel the raw mangoes.
- For the tempering, heat the oil and add the mustard seeds, fenugreek seeds, asafoetida, cumin seeds, curry leaves, red chillies and turmeric powder.
- Stir it for ½ minute and then add the cut mangoes to it.
- Add the water and let it boil on low heat.
- Add the jaggery and salt and stir well till the jaggery melts. If required add additional red chilli powder.
- Allow it to cool and store it in a tight lid jar.

Mix Vegetables Loncha

- 10-12 ivy gourd (tondli)
- 1 vati cauliflower (phulkobi)
- 1 vati fresh green peas (vatana)
- 2 medium carrots (gaajar)
- 1 radish (mulaa) (only the white part)
- 5-6 green chillies
- 1 vati lime juice
- 2 inches ginger
- 1 packet ready-made loncha masala

For the tempering

- ½ vati salt
- ¾ vati oil
- ½ teaspoon mustard seeds
- ½ teaspoon asafoetida
- ½ teaspoon fenugreek seeds (methi seeds)

Cut all the vegetables into medium pieces and add salt to it. Set aside for a day.

The next day, add the loncha masala to it and set aside for a day.

The next day, for the tempering, heat the oil, add mustard seeds and asafoetida to it and allow it to cool and then add the fenugreek seeds to the tempering.

Once cooked, add the tempering to the pickle.

Mix well and once cooled store it in a tight lid jar.

Mirchi Kharda

- ¼ kg green chillies (hirvi mirchi)
- Juice of 2 limes
- ½ vati salt
- 2 inches ginger
- 1 teaspoon cumin seeds

Mix all the ingredients in a mixer till coarse, without adding any water.

Store in the refrigerator.

Mirchi Loncha

Variation 1

- ¼ kg green chillies (hirvi mirchi)
- ¾ vati salt
- 1 packet ready-made loncha masala
- Juice of 7-8 limes
- ½ vati oil
- ½ teaspoon mustard seeds
- ½ teaspoon asafoetida

Tip: *The chillies used for these two recipes are long and parrot green in colour.*

- Clean, dry and cut the chillies into small pieces.
- Add the salt and set aside for 5-6 hours.
- Then add the loncha masala and lime juice and set aside for another 5-6 hours.
- The next day, for the tempering, heat the oil, and add the mustard seeds and asafoetida. Allow the tempering to cool and then add the chilli mixture.
- Mix well and store in a tight lid jar.

Mirchi Loncha

Variation 2

- ½ kg long green chillies (hirvi mirchi)
- ¾ vati mustard seeds
- 2 vatis water, boiled and cooled
- ¼ teaspoon fenugreek seed powder (methi powder)
- 2 teaspoons turmeric powder
- 3-4 vatis salt
- Juice of 6 limes or ½ vati lime juice

For the tempering

½ vati oil

4 teaspoons asafoetida

1 teaspoon mustard seeds

- Wash and dry the chillies and cut them into small pieces.
- In a mixer, make a paste of mustard seeds and water.
- To the chilli, add the paste, fenugreek seed powder, turmeric powder, salt and lime juice.
- For the tempering, heat the oil, add the mustard seeds and asafoetida.
- Allow the tempering to cool and then add to the chilli mixture.
- Mix well and store in a tight lid jar.

Kutaachi Mirchi

Variation 1

- ¼ kg long green chillies (hirvi mirchi)
- ¼ vati oil
- 1½ teaspoons fenugreek seed powder
- ¼ kg mustard powder
- ½ teaspoon turmeric powder
- ½ teaspoon asafoetida
- Juice of 2 limes
- 2-3 teaspoons salt

Wash and dry the chillies and cut into medium pieces. Heat the oil, add the chillies and stir-fry for 30 seconds.

Add the fenugreek seed powder, mustard powder, turmeric powder and asafoetida, and boil well.

Allow it to cool. Add the lime juice and salt and mix it well.

Store in a tight lid jar.

Kutaachi Mirchi

Variation 2

- ¼ kg green chillies (hirvi mirchi)
- ¼ kg mustard powder
- 1½ teaspoons fenugreek seeds (methi seeds)
- 2-3 teaspoons salt
- Juice of 3 limes

For the tempering

- ¼ vati oil
- ½ teaspoon asafoetida
- ½ teaspoon turmeric powder

Wash and dry the chillies and cut them into small pieces.

In a mixer, add the split mustard seeds, fenugreek seeds and salt, to make a paste.

Add the paste to the chillies, then add the salt and mix well. Add lime juice.

For the tempering, heat the oil and add the asafoetida and turmeric powder. Once the tempering has cooled, add it to the mixture and mix well.

Store in a tight lid jar.

Chatni

Another important accessory to our meals and snacks is chatni. Without it, many recipes would be incomplete. There are two prominent types of chatnis – wet chatni, which has to be consumed quickly due to its short shelf life – and dry chatni, which can be stored and enjoyed for a long period of time. With a little creativity, chatnis can also be used as salad dressings.

Naaralachi Safed Chatni

1 vati grated fresh coconut (naaral)
2 green chillies (hirvi mirchi)
½ inch ginger
¼ teaspoon cumin seeds
1 teaspoon lime juice
¼ teaspoon salt
¼ teaspoon sugar
2-3 teaspoons water

Coarsely grind all the ingredients together in a mixer and use immediately.

Naaralachi Hirvi Chatni

1 vati grated fresh coconut (naaral)
2 green chillies (hirvi mirchi)
½ inch ginger
¼ teaspoon cumin seeds
¼ vati coriander stems
1 teaspoon lime juice
½ teaspoon salt
½ teaspoon sugar
2 teaspoons water

Grind all the ingredients together in a mixer and use immediately.

Naaralachi Kairi Chatni

- 1 vati grated fresh coconut (naaral)
- 2 pieces of raw mango (kairi)
- 2 green chillies
- ½ inch ginger
- ½ teaspoon cumin seeds
- 4-5 garlic cloves
- ½ teaspoon salt
- ½ teaspoon sugar
- 2 teaspoons water

- Grind all the ingredients together in a mixer and use immediately.

Kanda Kairi Chatka

- 1 vati chopped onion (kanda)
- 1 vati raw mango (kairi), peeled and cut into small pieces
- 5-6 red chillies
- ¼ teaspoon cumin seeds
- ½ vati shredded jaggery
- ½ teaspoon salt

- Grind all the ingredients together in a mixer and use immediately.

Pudina Kothimbir Chatni

1 vati fresh mint leaves (pudina)

1 vati coriander leaves with stems (kothimbir)

1 teaspoon lime juice

2 green chillies

¼ teaspoon cumin seeds

½ teaspoon salt

½ teaspoon sugar

Water, as required

Grind all the ingredients together, preferably without water, in a mixer.

Add water as required.

Bhajyanchya Saalichi Chatni

1 vati shredded ridge gourd skins
Or shredded bottle gourd skins
Or shredded red pumpkin skins
(bhajyanchya saali)

1 vati shredded skins of raw mango

½ teaspoon oil

4 green chillies

¼ vati freshly chopped coriander leaves

¼ vati white sesame seeds

¼ vati grated dry coconut

¼ teaspoon salt

¼ teaspoon sugar

Choose any one of the vegetable skin for this chutney.

Heat the oil and add the shredded vegetable skins, chillies, coriander leaves, white sesame seeds, shredded coconut, salt and sugar, and fry on low heat till it becomes crunchy.

Store in a tight lid jar.

Tip: *This chutney has shelf life of 8 days.*

Kacchyaa Tomatochi Chatni

- 2 green unripe tomatoes
- ½ vati roasted groundnuts
- 4 green chillies
- ¼ teaspoon salt
- ¼ teaspoon sugar

For the tempering

- ½ teaspoon oil
- 1 teaspoon mustard seeds
- 1 teaspoon cumin seeds
- 1 teaspoon asafoetida
- 1 teaspoon turmeric powder

- Grind all the ingredients together in a mixer.
- For the tempering, heat the oil, add the mustard seeds, asafoetida and turmeric powder.
- Add the tempering to the chutney and mix well.
- Use immediately.

Ukdalelya Kairichi Chatni

- 1 vati raw mango (kairi) pulp
- ½ vati jaggery
- ¼ teaspoon cumin seeds
- 3-4 red chillies
- ½ teaspoon salt

For the tempering

- 1 teaspoon oil
- ½ teaspoon mustard seeds
- ½ teaspoon asafoetida
- ½ teaspoon turmeric powder

- Grind together the mango pulp, jaggery, cumin seeds, red chillies and salt.
- For the tempering, heat the oil, add the mustard seeds, asafoetida and turmeric powder.
- Add to the chutney and mix well.

Chana Dal Chatni

1 vati soaked split Bengal gram (chana dal)

½ teaspoon cumin seeds

2 green chillies

½ inch ginger

½ vati finely chopped coriander leaves

1 teaspoon lime juice or 1 big piece raw mango

¼ teaspoon salt

¼ teaspoon sugar

1 teaspoon oil

½ teaspoon mustard seeds

½ teaspoon cumin seeds

Grind all the ingredients together and use immediately.

Chinchechi Chatni

1 vati fresh tamarind (chinch)

3-4 green chillies

¼ teaspoon cumin seeds

¼ teaspoon salt

¼ teaspoon sugar

Grind all the ingredients together and use immediately.

Karvandache Chatni

1 vati Bengal currant (karvandaa)

2-3 green chillies

½ inch ginger

¼ teaspoon salt

½ teaspoon sugar

½ teaspoon cumin seeds

Grind all the ingredients together and use immediately.

Kaccha Kelyaachi Chatni

- 1 unripe banana (kaccha kelaa)
- ½ teaspoon oil
- ¼ vati grated fresh coconut or ¼ vati groundnuts
- ¼ teaspoon cumin seeds
- 1 red chilli or green chilli
- ¼ teaspoon jaggery
- 1 teaspoon lime juice
- ½ teaspoon salt

- Peel the banana and cut into small pieces.
- Heat the oil and sauté the banana pieces on low heat.
- Cool and grind with the rest of the ingredients and use immediately.

Amsool (Kokum) Chatni

- 8-10 kokum rinds (amsool)
- ¼ vati water
- ¼ teaspoon cumin seeds
- ¼ teaspoon salt
- ¼ teaspoon jaggery
- ¼ inch ginger

- Soak the kokum rinds in warm water for 10 minutes.
- Add the rest of the ingredients to the kokum rinds. Grind and use immediately.

Kavathache Chatni

- Pulp of 1 wood apple (kavath)
- Jaggery, half the quantity of the wood apple pulp
- 1 teaspoon red chilli powder
- ½ teaspoon salt
- ¼ teaspoon cumin seeds

- Grind all the ingredients together, without water and use immediately.

Khajurachi Chatni

- 8-10 dates (khajur)
- 1 lemon-sized jaggery ball (gul)
- 1 teaspoon tamarind pulp
- ¼ teaspoon cumin seeds
- ¼ teaspoon coriander-cumin powder
- 1 teaspoon red chilli powder
- ¼ teaspoon salt
- ½ vati water

Deseed the dates.

Grind all the ingredients together and use immediately.

Avalyachi Chatni

- 8-10 Indian gooseberries (rai avala)
- 2 green chillies
- ¼ teaspoon cumin seeds
- ¼ inch ginger
- ½ teaspoon salt
- 1 teaspoon sugar

Deseed the gooseberries.

Grind all the ingredients together and refrigerate.

This chatni can be used for up to 8-10 days if stored well.

Tip: *Avala is also called rai avala.*

Lasun Chatni

- 1 vati dry coconut
- 1 vati garlic cloves
- 3-4 red chillies
- ½ teaspoon salt

Grind all the ingredients together coarsely and store it is a tight lid jar.

Shengdana Chatni

- 1 vati groundnuts (shengdane)
- 2 teaspoon red chilli powder
- 1 teaspoon cumin seeds
- 1 teaspoon salt

- Grind all the ingredients together coarsely and serve.

Tip: *You can replace the cumin seeds with garlic cloves or curry leaves.*

Karale Chatni

- 1 vati niger seeds (karale)
- 1 vati dry coconut
- ½ vati white sesame seeds or black sesame seeds
- ½ vati groundnuts
- 10-15 curry leaves
- 5-6 red chillies
- 8-10 garlic cloves
- ½ teaspoon salt
- ¼ teaspoon citric acid granules

- Grind all the ingredients together coarsely.
- Store in a tight lid jar.

Tip: *Karale are long slender black seeds that are easily available in the market.*

Kadipatta Chatni

- 4 vati curry leaves (kadipatta)
- ½ teaspoon oil
- ¼ vati dry coconut
- ¼ vati white sesame seeds or groundnuts, or both
- 4-5 red chillies
- ¼ teaspoon salt
- ¼ teaspoon chaat masala or citric acid powder

- Lightly sauté the curry leaves in oil for 2-3 minutes on low heat. Do not allow them to burn.
- Once cooled, grind all the ingredients together and store it in a tight lid jar.

Gaahti Chatni

¼ kg onions (kanda)

2 teaspoons oil

¼ kg red chillies

1 vati coriander seeds

10-12 cloves

10-12 black peppercorns

2 inches cinnamon

1 vati fennel seeds

1 teaspoon cumin seeds

1 teaspoon black cumin seeds

3-4 bay leaves

¼ kg garlic cloves

¼ vati dry coconut

1 teaspoon poppy seeds

1 teaspoon white sesame seeds

1 teaspoon fenugreek seeds (methi seeds)

Slice the onions vertically and fry them till they are crunchy, and set aside.

In the remaining oil roast the red chillies, coriander seeds, cloves, black peppercorns, cinnamon, fennel seeds, cumin seeds, black cumin seeds and bay leaves, till fragrant and slightly golden.

Roast the garlic cloves separately.

Cool and add the garlic cloves to the mixture.

Grind all the ingredients together and store in a tight lid jar.

Koshimbir, Raita and Bharit

These are an important component of nutrition and a balanced diet, and are like salads.

Even though authentic recipes are shared here, one can be very creative by adding their own unique twist.

Mulyacha Chatkaa

- 1 vati split Bengal gram (chana dal)
- 1 radish (mulaa), shredded
- 2-3 green chillies, cut into medium pieces
- ½ vati fresh stems of coriander
- ½ teaspoon cumin seeds
- 1 teaspoon lime juice
- ½ teaspoon salt
- ½ teaspoon sugar

For the tempering

- 2 teaspoons oil
- ½ teaspoon mustard seeds
- ½ teaspoon asafoetida

Soak the split Bengal gram in water for 2 hours and strain.

To the shredded radish, add the rest of the ingredients, except the tempering ingredients, and mix well.

For the tempering, heat the oil, add the mustard seeds and asafoetida.

Add it to the mixture, mix well and serve.

Kaakadi Koshimbir

- 2 small cucumbers (kaakadi)
- ¼ teaspoon cumin seeds
- 1 green chilli
- ¼ teaspoon salt
- ¼ teaspoon sugar
- ¼ vati coriander leaves
- ½ vati yoghurt
- ¼ teaspoon ghee

Wash the cucumbers and cut them very finely.

Crush the cumin seeds, green chilli, salt and sugar in a mortar and pestle.

Mix all the ingredients together and serve.

Khamang Kaakadi

- 2 cucumbers (kaakadi)
- 2 green chillies
- ¼ vati coriander leaves
- ½ vati coarsely pounded groundnuts
- 1 teaspoon lime juice
- ¼ teaspoon salt

For the tempering

- 1¼ teaspoons ghee
- ½ teaspoon cumin seeds

- Cut the cucumbers finely.
- Add the rest of the ingredients to the cucumbers, except for the ghee and cumin seeds.
- For the tempering, heat the ghee and add the cumin seeds.
- Add this to the mixture, mix well and serve.

Tomato-Kanda Koshimbir

- 1 medium tomato
- 1 medium onion (kanda)
- ¼ vati coarsely pounded groundnuts
- ¼ vati freshly chopped coriander
- 1-2 green chillies
- ¼ teaspoon salt
- ¼ teaspoon sugar

- Mix together all the ingredients and serve.

Tip: *Carrot, beetroot, capsicum, apple or pomegranate can be added for variation.*

Gaajar-Moong Dal Koshimbir

- ½ vati skinless split green gram (moong dal)
- 2 carrots (gaajar)
- ½ vati coriander leaves
- ¼ vati grated fresh coconut
- ¼ teaspoon salt
- ¼ teaspoon sugar

For the tempering

- ½ teaspoon oil
- ¼ teaspoon mustard seeds
- ¼ teaspoon asafoetida

Soak the green gram for one hour and strain it.

Wash and shred the carrots.

Mix all the ingredients except the tempering.

For the tempering, heat the oil, add the mustard seeds and asafoetida.

Add the tempering to the other ingredients, mix well and serve.

Pikalelyaa Kelyachi/ Peruchi Koshimbir

- 1 over ripened banana (kelaa) or guava (peru)
- 1 vati yoghurt
- 1 vati coriander leaves
- ¼ teaspoon salt
- ¼ teaspoon sugar

Cut the banana or guava into small pieces.

Mix together all the ingredients and serve.

Pachadi

- 1 onion, finely chopped
- 1 tomato, finely chopped
- ½ small cabbage, finely chopped
- ½ shredded carrot
- 1 teaspoon lime juice
- ¼ vati coriander leaves
- ¼ teaspoon salt
- ¼ teaspoon sugar

For the tempering

- 1 teaspoon oil
- ½ teaspoon mustard seeds
- ½ teaspoon asafoetida
- ½ teaspoon turmeric powder

- Mix all the ingredients together except the tempering ingredients.
- For the tempering, heat the oil, add the mustard seeds, asafoetida and turmeric powder.
- Add the tempering to the mixture, mix well and serve.

Laal Bhopala Bharit

- ¼ kg red pumpkin (laad bhopala)
- ¼ vati chopped coriander leaves
- 1 green chilli
- ¼ vati coarsely pounded groundnuts or grated fresh coconut
- ½ teaspoon salt
- ½ teaspoon sugar
- ½ vati yoghurt

- Peel the pumpkin and cut it into small pieces. Boil, strain, and cool the pumpkin.
- Add the rest of the ingredients to the pumpkin.
- Mix well and serve cool.

Vaangyacha Dahi Bharit

- 1 fat and oblong brinjal (bharit vaangi)
- Oil, as required
- 1 onion, finely chopped
- ¼ vati coriander leaves
- 1 green chilli, finely chopped
- 1 teaspoon salt
- 1 teaspoon sugar
- ½ vati yoghurt

For the tempering

- 1 teaspoon oil
- ½ teaspoon mustard seeds
- ½ teaspoon asafoetida
- ½ teaspoon turmeric powder

Brush the brinjal with oil and roast it well from all sides on a gas flame. Cool and remove the pulp.

To the pulp, add the onion, coriander, chilli, salt and sugar. Whisk the yoghurt and add to the mixture.

For the tempering, heat the oil, add the mustard seeds, asafoetida and turmeric powder.

Add the tempering to the mixture. Mix well and serve.

Vaangyacha Kanda Tomato Bharit

- 1 fat and oblong brinjal (bharit vaangi)
- Oil, as required
- 1 small onion, chopped
- 1 green chilli, chopped
- 1 small tomato, chopped
- ¼ vati coriander leaves
- 1 teaspoon sugar
- 1 teaspoon salt

For the tempering

- 1 teaspoon oil
- ½ teaspoon mustard seeds
- ½ teaspoon asafoetida
- ½ teaspoon turmeric powder

Brush the brinjal with oil and roast it well from all sides on a gas flame.

Cool and remove the pulp and add the rest of the ingredients except for the tempering ingredients.

For the tempering, heat the oil, add the mustard seeds, asafoetida and turmeric powder.

Add the tempering to the mixture. Mix well and serve.

Tip: Bharit vaangi are big, fat, purple or black brinjals, that are easily available.

Vaangyacha Partun Bharit

- 1 fat and oblong brinjal (bharit vaangi)
- Oil, as required
- 1 green chilli, finely chopped
- ½ teaspoon turmeric powder
- ½ teaspoon red chilli powder
- 1 small onion, chopped
- 1 small tomato, chopped
- 1 small potato, chopped
- 1 vati fresh green peas
- ¼ vati coriander leaves
- ½ teaspoon salt
- ½ teaspoon sugar
- ¼ vati grated fresh coconut

For the tempering

- 2 teaspoons oil
- ½ teaspoon mustard seeds
- ½ teaspoon cumin seeds
- ½ teaspoon asafoetida

- Brush the brinjal with oil and roast it well from all sides on a gas flame.
- For the tempering, heat the oil and add the mustard seeds, cumin seeds and asafoetida.
- Add green chilli, turmeric powder, red chilli powder and stir it for half a minutes.
- Add the onion, tomato and potato and stir for another minute.
- Add the peas and cook covered, for another minute.
- Add the pulp of the brinjal and stir it well.
- Cook covered for a minute, add coriander leaves and remove from heat.
- Add the salt, sugar and grated coconut, mix well and serve.

Vaangyacha Chinch Gul Bharit

- 1 fat and oblong brinjal (bharit vaangi)
- Oil, as required
- 1 lemon-sized tamarind ball
- Water, as required
- 1 lemon-sized jaggery ball
- ½ teaspoon red chilli powder
- ¼ vati coriander leaves
- ¼ vati grated fresh coconut
- 1 teaspoon salt
- ¼ coarsely pounded groundnuts

For the tempering

- 1 teaspoon oil
- ¼ teaspoon cumin seeds

Brush the brinjal with oil and roast it well from all sides on a gas flame.

Cool and remove the pulp.

Add the tamarind to some water and make a pulp.

To the pulp, add all the other ingredients, except the tempering ingredients.

For the tempering, heat the oil and add the cumin seeds.

Add the tempering to the mixture. Mix well and serve.

Vaangyacha Naaral Bharit

- 1 fat and oblong brinjal (bharit vaangi)
- Oil, as required
- 1 green chilli
- ¼ vati coriander leaves
- ¼ coarsely pounded groundnuts
- 1 teaspoon salt
- 1 teaspoon sugar
- 1 vati coconut milk

Brush the brinjal with oil and roast it well from all sides on a gas flame.

Cool and remove the pulp. Chop the chilli, finely chop the coriander leaves and add to the pulp.

Add the coarsely pounded groundnuts, salt, sugar and the coconut milk. Mix well and serve.

Aluchyaa Dethincha Bharit

- 1 vati colocasia stems (aluchyaa dethi)
- 1 vati yoghurt
- 1 teaspoon coarsely pounded groundnuts
- 1 green chilli, finely chopped
- ½ teaspoon salt
- ½ teaspoon sugar

For the tempering

- 1 teaspoon oil
- ½ teaspoon mustard seeds
- ½ teaspoon asafoetida
- ½ teaspoon turmeric powder

- Peel the skin of the stems. Wash them well and cut into small pieces. Boil them in water. Strain and cool them.
- Add the remaining ingredients to the stems, except for the tempering ingredients.
- For the tempering, heat the oil, add the mustard seeds, asafoetida and turmeric powder.
- Add the tempering to the mixture.
- Mix well and serve.

Batatyache Bharit

- 1 medium potato (batata)
- 1 vati yoghurt
- ¼ teaspoon salt
- ¼ vati onions, finely chopped
- 2-4 garlic cloves, finely chopped
- ¼ vati coriander leaves
- ¼ teaspoon red chilli powder
- ¼ teaspoon sugar

- Boil the potato.
- Cool and cut into small pieces.
- Add the remaining ingredients to it.
- Stir well and serve.

Metkut/Dangar

- 2 tablespoons metkut or dangar
- 1 vati sweet yoghurt (dahi)
- ¼ teaspoon salt
- ¼ vati onion, finely chopped
- ¼ vati coriander leaves
- ¼ teaspoon red chilli powder
- ¼ teaspoon sugar

Mix all the ingredients together and serve.

Tip: *You can also add a tempering of oil and 5-6 curry leaves to this dish.*

Amba Dal

- 1 vati split Bengal gram (chana dal)
- 1 medium raw mango (kairi)
- 2 green chillies
- ½ teaspoon cumin seeds
- ½ vati coriander leaves
- ½ teaspoon salt
- ½ teaspoon sugar

For the tempering

- 2-3 teaspoons oil
- ½ teaspoon mustard seeds
- ½ teaspoon asafoetida
- ½ teaspoon turmeric powder
- 8-10 curry leaves

Soak the split Bengal gram for 2-3 hours and strain.

Wash, dry and shred the mango with the skin.

Crush the chillies, cumin seeds in a mortar and pestle. Add the coriander leaves, salt, sugar and shredded mango to the mixture, stir well.

For the tempering, heat the oil, add the mustard seeds, asafoetida, turmeric powder and curry leaves.

Add the tempering to the mixture.

Mix well and serve.

Panchaamrut

- 1 vati chopped green chillies
- 7-8 curry leaves
- 1 vati sliced dried coconut
- 1 vati cashew nuts
- 1 vati coarsely pounded sesame seeds
- 1 vati coarsely pounded groundnuts
- Lemon-sized tamarind ball soaked in water
- 2-3 teaspoons godaa masala
- 2-3 teaspoons coriander-cumin powder
- 1 teaspoon red chilli powder
- 2 tablespoons jaggery
- 1 teaspoon salt

For the tempering

- ½ vati oil
- 1teaspoon mustard seeds
- 1 teaspoon asafoetida
- 1 teaspoon turmeric powder

- For the tempering, heat the oil, add the mustard seeds, asafoetida and turmeric powder.
- Add the green chillies, curry leaves, coconut slices and fry till brown.
- Add the cashew nuts, pounded sesame seeds, pounded groundnuts, tamarind pulp and boil.
- Add the godaa masala, coriander-cumin powder, red chilli powder, jaggery and salt.
- Boil till the mixture thickens.
- Cool and serve.

Bhaji and Vade

These are fried crunchy snacks that are added to a meal. Enjoyed in every home on a rainy day with tea or coffee, or always perpared for a puja meal, there are many delicious recipes to choose from.

Bhaajni Vade

- 2 vatis Thalipeeth Bhaajni flour (page 10)
- 1 teaspoon carom seeds
- 1 teaspoon cumin seeds
- ½ teaspoon red chilli powder
- Salt to taste
- 2-3 green chillies
- ¼ teaspoon asafoetida
- ¼ teaspoon turmeric powder
- Water, as required
- Oil for deep-frying

- To the flour, add all the ingredients and water, and knead to make a firm dough.
- Make a small ball of the dough and flatten it with your palm on a fresh banana leaf or plastic sheet. Make a small hole right in the centre.
- Heat the oil and deep-fry the vade.
- Serve hot with dahi or loni.

Mixed Dal Vade

- 1 vati split Bengal gram (chana dal)
- ½ vati skinless split green gram (moong dal)
- ½ vati skinless split black gram (udid dal)
- ½ vati split red lentils (masoor dal)
- ½ inch ginger
- 2-3 green chillies
- ¼ vati coriander leaves
- Salt to taste
- Oil for deep-frying

- Soak all the grams and lentils for 5-6 hours. Strain and preserve the water as it can be used while grinding the grams and lentils.
- To the grams and lentils, add all the other ingredients and grind coarsely with minimum water.
- Make a small ball of the dough and flatten it with your palm on a fresh banana leaf or plastic sheet. Make a small hole right in the centre.
- Heat the oil and deep-fry the vade.
- Serve hot with chutneys or sauce.

Tip: *You can add shredded carrot, cabbage or radish to the mixture for variation.*

Udid Dal Vade

1 vati skinless split black gram (udid dal)

½ vati split Bengal gram (chana dal)

½ inch ginger

¼ vati grated fresh coconut

2 green chillies

Salt to taste

Oil for deep-frying

Follow the same method as the previous recipe.

Serve hot.

Moong Dal Bhaji

1 vati skinless split green gram (moong dal)

½ inch ginger

3 green chillies

½ teaspoon fennel seeds (badishep)

Salt to taste

Water, as required

1 big onion, finely chopped

¼ vati coriander leaves, finely chopped

Oil for deep-frying

Soak the green gram for 5-6 hours and strain.

To the green gram, add the ginger, chillies, fennel seeds and salt, and coarsely grind with minimum water.

To this mixture, add the onion and coriander leaves, and mix well. Follow the same method as in previous recipe.

Serve hot.

Kanda Bhaji

- 2 onions (kanda)
- 1 teaspoon salt
- Gram flour, as required
- ½ teaspoon red chilli powder
- 1 teaspoon semolina
- Oil for deep-frying

Tips:

- *Gram flour should be added as a binding agent so that the mixture can be moulded together to form small balls.*
- *To make the kanda/batata bhaji even more crisp, add 2 tablespoons rice flour to the gram flour.*

- Slice the onions vertically. Add the salt, cover and set aside for a while. After sometime the onions will release water, add the chilli powder, semolina and gram flour.
- Do not add water, unless required.
- The mixture should be mouldable by hand. Wait for 10-15 minutes and then make small balls by hand.
- Heat the oil and deep-fry the balls. Serve hot.

Batata Bhaji

- 2 big potatoes (batata)
- 1½ vati gram flour
- ¼ teaspoon carom seeds
- ½ teaspoon red chilli powder
- ¼ teaspoon turmeric powder
- ¼ teaspoon asafoetida
- Salt to taste
- Water, as required
- Oil for deep-frying

- Peel the potatoes, and cut into thin round slices. Soak them in salt water or they will turn black.
- Mix together all the other ingredients with water to make a thick batter. Add 1 teaspoon of hot oil to the batter. Heat the oil. Dip each potato slice in the batter and deep-fry. Serve hot.

Tips:

- *The batter consistency can be adjusted as required.*
- *A similar bhaji can be made with spinach, brinjal, carom leaves, cauliflower or banana.*
- *Adding hot oil to the batter makes the bhaji crispy.*

Vaanga Kaap

1 black, fat and oblong brinjal (bharit vaanga)

Salt to taste

1 vati gram flour

½ vati rice flour

2 teaspoon semolina

½ teaspoon red chilli powder

½ teaspoon turmeric powder

¼ teaspoon asafoetida

Oil for frying

Wash and dry the brinjal and cut into round slices uniformly.

Mix together all the other ingredients and then add the brinjal slices to it.

Allow the brinjal slices to marinate in this mixture and then coat them well with it on both sides.

Heat the oil and fry the kaap.

Serve hot.

Bhaaji and Palebhaaji

Vegetables are one of the most important components of our diet. In Brahmin cuisine, these are cooked in a way that the flavour, colour and the nutritional components of the bhaaji (vegetable) and palebhaaji (leafy vegetable) are preserved, and one can enjoy the dish at its the best. This is very unique and done only by this community, so enjoy these secret recipes!

Batata Kachryaa

- ¼ kg potatoes (batata)
- 2 green chillies
- 4-5 curry leaves
- ½ teaspoon chilli powder
- ¼ teaspoon sugar
- Salt to taste
- 1 vati coriander leaves

For the tempering

- 2 teaspoons oil
- ¼ teaspoon mustard seeds
- ¼ teaspoon asafoetida
- ¼ teaspoon turmeric powder

Peel the potatoes, cut them into 4 parts and then cut them into thin slices.

Soak them in salt water or they will turn black.

For the tempering, heat the oil, add the mustard seeds, asafoetida and turmeric powder.

Add the green chillies and curry leaves and toss for 30 seconds.

Add the sliced potatoes and cook covered for a minute.

Add the red chilli powder, sugar and salt and cook covered for one minute on low heat.

Garnish with the coriander leaves and serve hot.

Ukdalelya Batata Bhaaji

- ¼ kg potatoes (batata)
- Salt to taste
- ¼ teaspoon sugar
- 1 teaspoon lime juice
- ¼ vati coriander leaves

For the tempering

- 1 teaspoon oil
- ¼ teaspoon mustard seeds
- ½ teaspoon cumin seeds
- ¼ teaspoon asafoetida
- ½ teaspoon turmeric powder
- ¼ inch ginger, chopped
- 2 green chillies, finely chopped
- 4-5 curry leaves

- Boil the potatoes, peel and cut them into 1-inch medium pieces.
- For the tempering, heat the oil, add the mustard seeds, cumin seeds, asafoetida, turmeric powder, ginger, green chillies and curry leaves and stir for a minute.
- Add the potatoes, salt, sugar and lime juice, and toss it well on low heat.
- Garnish with the coriander leaves and serve.

Tip: *Grated fresh coconut can also be added.*

Batatyaacha Rassa

- ¼ kg boiled potatoes (batata)
- ¼ kg grated fresh coconut
- 2 green chillies
- 1 inch ginger
- 1 medium tomato
- Salt to taste
- ¼ teaspoon sugar
- ¼ vati coriander leaves

For the tempering

- ¼ teaspoon oil
- ¼ teaspoon mustard seeds
- ¼ teaspoon cumin seeds
- ¼ teaspoon asafoetida
- ¼ teaspoon turmeric powder
- 4-5 curry leaves

Cut the boiled potatoes into medium pieces.

Grind together the coconut, green chillies, ginger and tomato.

For the tempering, heat the oil, add the mustard seeds, cumin seeds, asafoetida, turmeric powder and curry leaves.

Add the potatoes, toss them well and cook covered for a minute.

Add the ground mixture and a little warm water and cook covered for a minute.

Add the salt and sugar and allow it to boil.

Garnish with the coriander leaves and serve hot.

Sansari Batata/ Goti Batata Rassa

- ¼ kg baby potatoes (goti batata)
- 1 small onion
- ¼ vati grated fresh coconut
- 2 green chillies
- 1 inch ginger
- 2 cloves
- 2 black peppercorns
- ¼ inch cinnamon
- 2 red chillies
- 1 teaspoon jaggery
- Small ball of tamarind
- Salt to taste
- Warm water, as required
- ¼ vati coriander leaves

For the tempering

- ¼ teaspoon oil
- ¼ teaspoon mustard seeds
- ¼ teaspoon asafoetida
- ¼ teaspoon turmeric powder

- Boil the potatoes and peel them. Cut the onion into medium pieces.
- Grind together the fresh coconut, green chillies and ginger.
- For the tempering, heat the oil, add the mustard seeds, asafoetida and turmeric powder.
- Add the cloves, peppercorns, cinnamon and red chillies, and stir for a minute.
- Add the onions and toss well. Add the boiled potatoes and toss again.
- Add the ground masala, jaggery, tamarind, salt and some warm water.
- Cook covered and allow it to boil on low heat.
- Garnish with the coriander leaves and serve hot.

Tondlyachi Bhaaji

- ¼ kg small slender ivy gourd (tondli)
- ¼ teaspoon red chilli powder
- ¼ vati grated fresh coconut or coarsely pounded groundnuts
- ¼ teaspoon sugar
- ¼ teaspoon salt

For the tempering

- 1 teaspoon oil
- ¼ teaspoon mustard seeds
- ¼ teaspoon asafoetida
- ¼ teaspoon turmeric powder

Wash and dry the ivy gourd. Cut them vertically or slice them horizontally into thin slices.

For the tempering, heat the oil, add the mustard seeds, asafoetida and turmeric powder.

Add the ivy gourd, toss well and cook covered for a minute.

Add the red chilli powder, grated coconut or pounded groundnuts, sugar and salt, and cook covered again on low heat, till the bhaaji is done.

Serve hot.

Masala Tondli

- 1 kg small slender ivy gourd (tondli)
- Warm water, as required
- 1 teaspoon godaa masala
- 1 teaspoon coriander-cumin powder
- 1 teaspoon red chilli powder
- Lemon-sized tamarind ball
- 1 tablespoon jaggery
- ¼ vati coarsely pounded groundnuts
- Salt to taste
- ¼ vati coriander leaves
- ¼ vati grated fresh coconut

For the tempering

- 1 teaspoon oil
- ½ teaspoon mustard seeds
- ½ teaspoon cumin seeds
- ½ teaspoon asafoetida
- ½ teaspoon turmeric powder

- Wash and dry the ivy gourd and slice them vertically.
- For the tempering, heat the oil and add mustard seeds, cumin seeds, asafoetida and turmeric powder.
- Add the ivy gourd and toss well.
- Add some warm water, as per the desired consistency and cook covered for a minute.
- Add the godaa masala, coriander-cumin powder, red chilli powder, tamarind, jaggery, coarsely pounded groundnuts and salt.
- Cook covered again, till it boils and the bhaaji is done.
- Garnish with the coriander leaves and coconut. Serve hot.

Padwalachi Bhaaji

¼ kg snake gourds (padwal)

¼ split field beans (val dal) or skinless split green gram (moong dal) or chana dal (split Bengal gram)

¼ vati grated fresh coconut

½ teaspoon cumin seeds

2 green chillies, slit

½ teaspoon coriander-cumin powder

Salt to taste

1 teaspoon sugar

Water, as required

¼ vati coriander leaves

For the tempering

1 teaspoon oil

½ teaspoon mustard seeds

½ teaspoon asafoetida

½ teaspoon turmeric powder

Wash and dry the snake gourds and cut them into medium size cubes.

Choose the dal you would like, soak it for an hour and strain.

Grind together the coconut, cumin seeds, and 1 green chilli.

For the tempering, heat the oil, add the mustard seeds, asafoetida, and turmeric powder.

Add 1 green chilli and the soaked dal, mix and cook covered for a minute.

Add the snake gourd and some warm water. Cook covered again for a minute.

Add the ground masala, coriander-cumin powder, salt, sugar and water as required, and allow it to boil, till the bhaaji is well done. Serve hot.

Bharlele Padwal

- ¼ kg snake gourd (padwal)
- ¼ vati grated fresh coconut
- ¼ vati coarsely pounded groundnuts
- 1 teaspoon red chilli powder
- 1 teaspoon coriander-cumin powder
- ¼ vati finely chopped coriander leaves
- 1 teaspoon lime juice
- ½ teaspoon salt
- ½ teaspoon sugar
- Warm water, as required
- ¼ vati coriander leaves

For the tempering

- 1 teaspoon oil
- ½ teaspoon mustard seeds
- ½ teaspoon asafoetida
- ½ teaspoon turmeric powder

- Wash the snake gourds and slit them vertically in such a way that they can be stuffed with masala.
- Mix together the coconut, pounded groundnuts, red chilli powder, coriander-cumin powder, coriander leaves, lime juice, salt, and sugar.
- Stuff the slit snake gourds with this masala.
- For the tempering, heat the oil, add mustard seeds, asafoetida, turmeric powder.
- Add the stuffed snake gourds one by one, if any masala is leftover add that too and cook covered.
- If required add some warm water and cook on low heat for 5-6 minutes, till the bhaaji is done.
- Garnish with the coriander leaves and serve hot.

Kaarylachee Bhaaji

- ¼ kg bitter gourds (kaarli)
- 1 teaspoon salt + to taste
- 2 cups water
- ½ teaspoon red chilli powder
- ¼ vati coarsely pounded groundnuts
- 1 teaspoon jaggery
- 1 teaspoon lime juice
- ¼ vati coriander leaves
- ¼ vati grated fresh coconut

For the tempering

- 2 teaspoons oil
- ¼ teaspoon mustard seeds
- ¼ teaspoon asafoetida
- ¼ turmeric powder

Wash and dry the bitter gourds and cut them into medium pieces.

Rub them with 1 teaspoon salt and set aside for 30 minutes, then strain all the liquid released from the bitter gourds. This reduces their bitterness.

Boil the bitter gourds in 2 cups of water, for 5 minutes on low heat and strain.

For the tempering, heat the oil, add the mustard seeds, asafoetida, and turmeric powder.

Add the red chilli powder, pounded groundnuts, salt, jaggery, lime juice, coriander leaves and coconut. Cook till the bhaaji is done.

Serve hot.

Tip: *This is a dry bhaaji and tastes best when prepared with coarsely pounded groundnuts (dana kut). Coarsely pounded sesame seeds (til kut) can also be added to enhance the taste.*

Kaarlyaachi Chinch Gul Bhaaji

- ¼ kg bitter gourds (kaarli)
- 2 big onions
- 2 big tomatoes
- ½ teaspoon red chilli powder
- ½ teaspoon dry ginger powder
- ½ teaspoon turmeric powder
- 1 teaspoon tamarind pulp (chinch)
- 2 teaspoons jaggery (gul)
- ½ teaspoon salt
- Warm water, as required
- ¼ vati coriander leaves

For the tempering

- 1 teaspoon oil
- 1 teaspoon mustard seeds
- 1 teaspoon cumin seeds
- 1 teaspoon fennel seeds
- 1 teaspoon Nigella seeds
- 1 teaspoon fenugreek seeds (methi seeds)

- Cut the bitter gourds and onions into medium pieces.
- Purée the tomatoes.
- For the tempering, heat the oil, add the mustard seeds, cumin seeds, fennel seeds, Nigella seeds and fenugreek seeds.
- Add the onions and bitter gourds, and toss well.
- Add the tomato purée, red chilli powder, dry ginger powder, turmeric powder, tamarind pulp, jaggery, salt, warm water if required, and cook covered, till done.
- Garnish with the coriander leaves and serve hot.

Bharleli Kaarli

- ¼ kg bitter gourds (kaarli)
- 1½ teaspoons salt
- 2 cups water
- 1 teaspoon red chilli powder
- 1 teaspoon coriander-cumin powder
- 1 teaspoon godaa masala
- ¼ vati coarsely pounded groundnuts
- ¼ grated fresh coconut
- ¼ vati coriander leaves, chopped
- Lemon-sized jaggery ball
- 1 teaspoon lime juice

For the tempering

- 2 teaspoons oil
- ¼ teaspoon mustard seeds
- ¼ teaspoon asafoetida
- ½ turmeric powder

Cut the bitter gourds into two parts horizontally and then slit each part in such a way that they can be stuffed with masala.

Rub them with 1 teaspoon salt and set aside for 30 minutes, then strain all the liquid released from the bitter gourds. This reduces their bitterness.

Boil them in 2 cups of water, for 5 minutes on low heat and strain.

Mix together the red chilli powder, coriander-cumin powder, godaa masala, pounded groundnuts, coconut, coriander leaves, salt, jaggery, and lime juice, and mix well.

Stuff the bitter gourds with this masala.

For the tempering, heat the oil, add the mustard seeds, asafoetida and turmeric powder.

Add the bitter gourds, one by one and cook covered on low heat.

Add some warm water if required, and cook for 5-6 minutes till the done.

Serve hot.

Shahi Kaarli

- ¼ kg bitter gourds (kaarli)
- ½ teaspoon salt
- 1 teaspoon oil
- ½ teaspoon fennel seeds
- 2 medium onions, finely chopped
- 10-12 raisins
- 10- 12 cashew nuts
- ½ teaspoon tamarind pulp
- Lemon-sized jaggery ball
- ½ teaspoon red chilli powder
- ½ teaspoon turmeric powder
- ¼ vati coarsely pounded groundnuts
- ¼ vati grated fresh coconut
- ¼ vati coriander leaves

- Cut the bitter gourds horizontally, into thin slices.
- Rub them with salt and set aside for 30 minutes, then strain all the liquid released from the bitter gourds. This reduces their bitterness.
- Heat the oil and add the fennel seeds.
- Add the bitter gourds and toss them well for a minute.
- Add the rest of the ingredients except for the coriander leaves and coconut.
- Sauté them well and cook covered for a minute, till done.
- Garnish with the coconut and coriander leaves and serve hot.

Gavaar Laal Bhopala Bhaaji

- ¼ kg cluster beans (gavaar)
- ¼ kg red pumpkin (bhopala)
- Warm water, as required
- 1 teaspoon red chilli powder
- 1 teaspoon coriander-cumin powder
- 1 teaspoon godaa masala
- ¼ teaspoon jaggery
- Salt to taste
- ¼ vati grated fresh coconut

For the tempering

- 1 teaspoon oil
- ¼ teaspoon carom seeds
- ½ teaspoon mustard seeds
- ½ teaspoon asafoetida
- ½ teaspoon turmeric powder

Cut the cluster beans into small pieces. Cut the red pumpkin into medium pieces.

For the tempering, heat the oil, add the carom seeds, mustard seeds, asafoetida and turmeric powder.

Add the cluster beans, mix well and cook covered. Add warm water as required.

After a couple of minutes add the red pumpkin and cook covered for another minute.

Add the red chilli powder, coriander-cumin powder, godaa masala, jaggery and salt. Cook on low heat, till done.

Garnish with grated coconut and serve hot.

Tip: *Adding carom seeds makes the bhaji more flavourful and easy to digest.*

Laal Bhoplyaachi Bhaaji

- ¼ kg red pumpkin (laal bhopala)
- 1 green chilli, slit
- ½ teaspoon fenugreek seeds (methi seeds)
- ¼ teaspoon coriander-cumin powder
- Salt to taste
- ½ teaspoon sugar
- ¼ vati grated fresh coconut
- Coriander leaves, as required (optional)

For the tempering

- 1 teaspoon oil
- ¼ teaspoon mustard seeds
- ¼ teaspoon asafoetida
- ¼ teaspoon turmeric powder

- Peel the thick outer skin of the red pumpkin and cut it into medium pieces.
- For the tempering, heat the oil and add mustard seeds, asafoetida, and turmeric powder.
- Add the green chilli and fenugreek seeds, mix well and cook covered for a minute.
- Add coriander-cumin powder, salt and sugar, and cook for a couple of minutes. This bhaaji cooks quickly, so check on it.
- Garnish with grated coconut and coriander leaves.
- Serve hot.

Farasbeechi Bhaaji

- ½ kg French beans (farasbeech)
- ¼ vati grated fresh coconut
- 2 green chillies, slit
- 1 teaspoon oil
- ½ teaspoon cumin seeds
- Salt to taste
- ¼ teaspoon jaggery

- Cut off the tips and de-string the French beans. Wash them well and cut into small pieces.
- Grind together the coconut and 1 green chilli coarsely.
- Heat the oil, add the cumin seeds, 1 green chilli and French beans, and cook covered for a minute.
- Add the ground masala, coriander-cumin powder, salt and jaggery. Add warm water if required, and cook, till done. Serve hot.

Ghevdyachee Bhaaji

- ¼ kg dolichos beans (ghevda)
- 1 medium potato
- ¼ teaspoon red chilli powder
- 1 teaspoon coriander-cumin powder
- 1 teaspoon godaa masala
- ¼ teaspoon jaggery
- 2-3 teaspoon coarsely pounded groundnuts
- Salt to taste
- Warm water, as required
- ¼ vati grated fresh coconut

For the tempering

- 1 teaspoon oil
- ¼ teaspoon mustard seeds
- ¼ teaspoon asafoetida
- ¼ teaspoon turmeric powder

Cut off the tips and de-string the dolichos beans.

Wash them well and break then into medium pieces. Cut the potatoes in small pieces.

For the tempering, heat the oil, add the mustard seeds, asafoetida and turmeric powder.

Add the dolichos beans and potatoes, mix well and cook covered for a minute.

Add the red chilli powder, coriander-cumin powder, godaa masala, jaggery, pounded groundnuts and salt, and cook covered on low heat. Add warm water if required, and cook, till done.

Garnish with grated coconut and serve hot.

Sankrant Mixed Bhaaji

- ¼ kg dolichos beans (ghevda)
- ¼ kg fresh field beans
- 1 carrot
- 1 drumstick
- 1 medium potato
- 1 small brinjal
- ½ vati warm water
- 1 teaspoon red chilli powder
- 1 teaspoon turmeric powder
- 1 teaspoon godaa masala
- 1 teaspoon coriander-cumin powder
- ½ teaspoon jaggery
- 2 teaspoons coarsely pounded groundnuts
- 1 teaspoon coarsely pounded sesame seeds
- Salt to taste
- ¼ vati grated fresh coconut

For the tempering

- 1 teaspoon oil
- ½ teaspoon mustard seeds
- ½ teaspoon asafoetida
- ½ teaspoon turmeric powder

- Cut off the tips and de-string the dolichos beans.
- Soak the field beans in water.
- Cut the carrot, drumsticks, potato and brinjal into medium pieces.
- For the tempering, heat the oil, add the mustard seeds, asafoetida and turmeric powder.
- Add all the vegetables one by one, mix well and cook covered.
- Add ½ vati warm water to it and allow it to cook.
- Add the red chilli powder, turmeric powder, godaa masala, coriander-cumin powder, jaggery, pounded groundnuts, pounded sesame seeds and salt.
- Add water if required, and cook covered on low heat for 5-6 minutes, till done.
- Garnish with the grated coconut and serve hot.

Tip: *1 slit green chilli can be added to the tempering.*

Suranachi Bhaaji

- ¼ kg white elephant foot yam (suran)
- Warm water, as required
- 2 kokum rinds
- ¼ vati grated fresh coconut
- 2 green chillies, slit
- ¼ teaspoon cumin seeds
- ¼ inch ginger
- ½ teaspoon jaggery
- ¼ vati coarsely pounded groundnuts
- Salt to taste
- ¼ coriander leaves

For the tempering

- 1 teaspoon oil
- ¼ teaspoon mustard seeds
- ¼ teaspoon asafoetida
- ¼ teaspoon turmeric powder

Wash and clean the yam and cut into medium pieces.

Boil them in water along with the kokum for 2-3 minutes and strain.

Grind together the coconut, 1 green chilli, cumin seeds and ginger together.

For the tempering, heat the oil, add the mustard seeds, asafoetida and turmeric powder.

Add 1 green chilli, mix well. Add the yam, ground masala, jaggery, pounded groundnuts and salt.

Cook for 2-3 minutes on low heat, till done.

Garnish with the coriander leaves and serve hot.

Dudhi Bhopala Bhaaji

- ¼ kg bottle gourd (dudhi bhopala)
- ¼ vati split Bengal gram (chana dal) or skinless split green gram (moong dal)
- ¼ vati grated fresh coconut
- 2 green chillies, slit
- ¼ teaspoon cumin seeds
- ¼ inch ginger
- ¼ teaspoon coriander-cumin powder
- ¼ teaspoon sugar
- Salt to taste
- Warm water, as required
- ¼ vati coriander leaves

For the tempering

- 1 teaspoon oil
- ¼ teaspoon mustard seeds
- ¼ teaspoon asafoetida
- ¼ teaspoon turmeric powder

- Wash and peel the bottle gourd and cut into medium pieces.
- Soak the grams for 30 minutes.
- Grind together the coconut, 1 green chilli and cumin seeds coarsely.
- For the tempering, heat the oil, add the mustard seeds, asafoetida and turmeric powder.
- Add 1 green chilli and the soaked dal, mix well and cook covered for a minute.
- Add the bottle gourd, coriander-cumin powder, sugar, salt, warm water if required, and cook, till done.
- Garnish with coriander leaves and serve hot.

Tip: *You can prepare koholaa, papaya and cucumber the same way.*

Kelphool Bhaaji

- 1 banana flower
- ½ vati buttermilk
- Water, as required
- ½ teaspoon salt + to taste
- 4-5 red chillies
- ½ vati skinless split green gram (moong dal)
- ½ teaspoon sugar
- ½ vati grated fresh coconut
- ½ vati coriander leaves

For the tempering

- 2 teaspoons oil
- ½ teaspoon mustard seeds
- ½ teaspoon cumin seeds
- ½ teaspoon asafoetida
- ½ teaspoon turmeric powder

Open the banana flower properly, remove the outer red skin. Retain the inner white core and the flower. Cut it into small pieces.

To the buttermilk, add the water and salt, and soak the banana flower in it for an hour.

Pressure cook this mixture till 3 whistles are released. Cool and strain.

For the tempering, heat the oil, add the mustard seeds, cumin seeds, asafoetida and turmeric powder.

Add the red chillies, stir well and then remove them from the tempering and set aside.

Then add the strained banana flower pieces, split green gram, sugar and salt, and mix well.

Crush the red chillies and add to the bhaaji.

Add the coconut and cook on low heat for 5-6 minutes, till done.

Garnish with coriander leaves and serve hot.

Phanasaachi Bhaaji

- 1 fresh jackfruit (phanas)
- ½ vati buttermilk
- 2-3 red chillies
- 1 vati soaked fresh green field beans (vaal beans)
- ½ teaspoon sugar
- ½ teaspoon salt
- ½ vati grated fresh coconut

For the tempering

- 2-3 teaspoons oil
- ½ teaspoon mustard seeds
- ½ teaspoon asafoetida
- ½ teaspoon turmeric powder

- Remove the green shell of the jackfruit and the white parts. Only use the inner core of the fruit and cut it into small pieces.
- Store the seeds (athale) of the jackfruit.
- Soak the jackfruit in buttermilk and water in a pressure cooker.
- Pressure cook this mixture till 3 whistles are released. Cool and strain.
- For the tempering, heat the oil, add the mustard seeds, asafoetida and turmeric powder.
- Add the red chillies, mix well and add the jackfruit pieces, field beans, sugar and salt.
- Mix well and cook covered for 5-6 minutes, till done.
- Garnish with grated coconut and serve hot.

Phanas Aathale Bhaaji

- ½ kg jackfruit (phanas) along with the seeds (aathale are the seeds of the jackfruit)
- 5-6 red chillies
- ½ vati cashew nuts
- ½ teaspoon sugar
- ½ teaspoon salt
- ¼ vati grated fresh coconut

For the tempering

- 2 teaspoons oil
- ½ teaspoon mustard seeds
- ½ teaspoon asafoetida
- ½ teaspoon turmeric powder

Clean the jackfruit seeds and pressure cook them till 3 whistles are released.

Cool and remove the outter cover of the seeds and crush some of them.

For the tempering, heat the oil, add the mustard seeds, asafoetida and turmeric powder.

Added the chillies, jackfruit seeds, cashew nuts, sugar, salt and cook for 5-6 minutes, till done.

Garnish with grated coconut and serve hot.

Parvarachi Bhaaji

- ¼ kg pointed gourd (parvar)
- ¼ teaspoon cumin seeds
- 2 green chillies
- 1 teaspoon coriander-cumin powder
- ¼ vati grated fresh coconut
- Salt to taste
- ¼ teaspoon sugar

For the tempering

- 1 teaspoon oil
- ¼ teaspoon mustard seeds
- ¼ teaspoon asafoetida
- ¼ teaspoon turmeric powder

Wash, dry and cut the pointed gourd into medium pieces.

Crush the cumin seeds and green chillies together.

For the tempering, heat the oil, add the mustard seeds, asafoetida and turmeric powder.

Add the crushed cumin seeds and chillies. Add the pointed gourd, mix well.

Add the coriander-cumin powder, coconut, salt, sugar and cook covered for 5-6 minutes, till done. Serve hot.

Bharli Vaanga

- ¼ kg small brinjals with thorny stems (kaateri vaangi)
- 1 onion, chopped
- 2 teaspoons coarsely pounded sesame seeds
- 2 teaspoons coarsely pounded groundnuts
- ¼ vati grated fresh coconut
- ¼ vati coriander leaves
- 1 teaspoon coriander-cumin powder
- 3 teaspoons godaa masala
- 1 teaspoon red chilli powder
- Lemon-sized tamarind ball
- 2 teaspoons jaggery
- Salt to taste

For the tempering

- 3 teaspoons oil
- ½ teaspoon mustard seeds
- ½ teaspoon asafoetida
- ½ teaspoon turmeric powder

- Wash and slit the brinjals into 4 pieces so that you can stuff them with masala. Do not remove the stems of the brinjals.
- Mix together the onion, pounded sesame seeds, pounded groundnuts, fresh coconut, coriander leaves, all the dry masalas, tamarind pulp, jaggery, salt and mix well. Stuff the brinjals with this prepared masala.
- For the tempering, heat the oil, add the mustard seeds, asafoetida and turmeric powder.
- Add the brinjals one by one, if any masala is left over, add it on top. Add warm water if required. Cook covered for 8-10 minutes on low heat, till done.
- Serve hot.

Tip: *You can also add 1 teaspoon fenugreek powder to the mixture of dry masalas.*

Vaanga Batata Bhaaji

¼ kg small brinjals with thorny stems (kaateri vaangi)

1 medium potato

Warm water, as required

½ teaspoon red chilli powder

2 teaspoons godaa masala

1 teaspoon coriander-cumin powder

2 teaspoons coarsely pounded groundnuts

2 teaspoons coarsely pounded sesame seeds

½ teaspoon jaggery

Salt to taste

For the tempering

2 teaspoons oil

¼ teaspoon mustard seeds

¼ teaspoon asafoetida

¼ teaspoon turmeric powder

Remove the stem and cut the brinjals into medium pieces.

Peel the potato, cut into medium pieces and soak both the vegetables in water.

For the tempering, heat the oil, add the mustard seeds, asafoetida and turmeric powder.

Add the vegetables and mix well. Cook covered for a couple of minutes, if required add warm water.

Add all the dry masalas, pounded groundnuts, pounded sesame seeds, jaggery and salt.

Cook covered for 4-5 minutes on low heat, till done and serve hot.

Navalkol Bhaaji

- ¼ kg kohlrabi (navalkol)
- 1 green chilli, chopped
- ¼ vati grated fresh coconut
- 1 teaspoon sugar
- Salt to taste

For the tempering

- 2 teaspoons oil
- ½ teaspoon mustard seeds
- ½ teaspoon asafoetida
- ½ teaspoon turmeric powder

- Wash and cut the kohlrabi into thin slices.
- For the tempering, heat the oil, add the mustard seeds, asafoetida and turmeric powder.
- Add the green chilli and vegetables. Cook covered for a couple of minutes.
- Add the coconut, sugar and salt and cook, till done.
- Serve hot.

Alkudi Kachryaa Bhaaji

- ½ kg taro root (alkudi/arbi)
- 2 green chillies, finely chopped
- 2-3 kokum rinds
- ¼ vati coarsely pounded groundnuts
- Salt to taste
- Sugar to taste

For the tempering

- 2 teaspoons ghee
- ½ teaspoon cumin seeds

- Clean, boil, peel and make thin slices of the taro root.
- For the tempering, heat the ghee and add the cumin seeds.
- Add the green chillies, sliced taro root and mix well.
- Cook covered for a couple of minutes. Add the kokum rinds.
- Add the pounded groundnuts, salt and sugar. Toss well and cook for another 2-3 minutes, till done.
- Serve hot.

Kobichi Bhaaji

¼ kg cabbage (kobi)

3-4 teaspoons split Bengal gram (chana dal)

¾ teaspoon grated fresh coconut

½ inch ginger

2 green chillies

Salt to taste

For the tempering

2 teaspoons oil

½ teaspoon mustard seeds

½ teaspoon asafoetida

½ teaspoon turmeric powder

Wash and cut the cabbage into thin slices. Soak the split Bengal gram for 2-3 hours.

Grind together the coconut, ginger and chillies coarsely.

For the tempering, heat the oil, add the mustard seeds, asafoetida and turmeric powder. Mix well and cook covered for 4-5 minutes on low heat.

Add the ground masala and salt, and cook, till done.

Serve hot.

Kobi Gaajar Bhaaji

¼ kg cabbage (kobi)

¼ kg carrot (gaajar)

1 green chilli

Salt to taste

¼ teaspoon sugar

For the tempering

2 teaspoons oil

½ teaspoon mustard seeds

½ teaspoon asafoetida

½ teaspoon turmeric powder

Wash and finely chop the cabbage. Shred the carrot.

For the tempering, heat the oil, add the mustard seeds, asafoetida and turmeric powder.

Add the chilli and vegetables and mix well.

Cook covered for 5-6 minutes. Sauté well, add salt and sugar.

Cook covered for another 5 minutes on low heat, till done.

Serve hot.

Cauliflower Bhaaji

- ¼ kg cauliflower (phulkobi)
- 3 teaspoons grated fresh coconut
- 1 green chilli
- ¼ teaspoon cumin seeds
- ½ inch ginger
- ¼ vati green peas
- Salt to taste
- 1 teaspoon lime juice
- 2 tablespoons coriander leaves

For the tempering

- 2 teaspoons oil
- ½ teaspoon mustard seeds
- ½ teaspoon asafoetida
- ½ teaspoon turmeric powder
- 1 green chilli, slit

- Wash the cauliflower and finely chop or shred it.
- Grind together the coconut, 1 green chilli, cumin seeds, and ginger coarsely.
- For the tempering, heat the oil, add the mustard seeds, asafoetida, turmeric powder and green chilli.
- Add the cauliflower and green peas and mix well.
- Cook covered for 5-6 minutes on low heat, till done.
- Add the salt and lime juice, and mix. Garnish with coriander leaves and serve hot.

Cauliflower Batata Vatana Bhaaji

- 1 vati cauliflower (phulkobi)
- 1 potato (batata)
- 1 vati green peas (vatana)
- 3 teaspoons grated fresh coconut
- Salt to taste
- 2 tablespoons coriander leaves

For the tempering

- 2 teaspoons oil
- ½ teaspoon mustard seeds
- ½ teaspoon asafoetida
- ½ teaspoon turmeric powder
- 1 green chilli, slit

- Cut the cauliflower into small pieces. Peel the potato and cut into small pieces.
- For the tempering, heat the oil, add the mustard seeds, asafoetida, turmeric powder and green chilli.
- Add the vegetables and coconut and mix well.
- Cook covered for 7-8 minute on low heat, till done.
- Garnish with coriander leaves and serve hot.

Shiraalyachi Bhaaji

- ½ kg ridge gourds (shiraali)
- 1 medium potato
- ½ teaspoon cumin seeds
- 3 teaspoons grated fresh coconut
- Salt to taste

For the tempering

- 2 teaspoons oil
- ½ teaspoon mustard seeds
- ½ teaspoon asafoetida
- ½ teaspoon turmeric powder
- 1 green chilli, slit

Peel the ridge gourds, cut into medium pieces and soak them in water.

Peel the potato, cut into medium pieces and soak them in water.

Grind together the cumin seeds and coconut coarsely.

For the tempering, heat the oil, add the mustard seeds, asafoetida, turmeric powder and green chilli.

Add the cut vegetables, mix well and cook covered. Add the ground masala and cook covered for 5-6 minutes on low heat, till done. Serve hot.

Shevgaa Shengaa Bhaaji

- 2-3 drumsticks (shevgaa sheng)
- Water, as required
- ½ teaspoon coriander-cumin powder
- ½ teaspoon godaa masala
- ½ teaspoon red chilli powder
- ¼ vati grated fresh coconut
- Salt to taste

For the tempering

- 2 teaspoons oil
- ½ teaspoon mustard seeds
- ½ teaspoon asafoetida
- ½ teaspoon turmeric powder

Peel the drumsticks, cut into 2 inches pieces and boil them in water.

For the tempering, heat the oil, add the mustard seeds, asafoetida and turmeric powder.

Add the drumsticks and ½ vati of warm water, in which the drumsticks were boiled.

Add the dry masalas, fresh coconut and salt. Cook on low heat for 5-6 minutes, till done. Serve hot.

Bhendichi Bhaaji

- ½ kg ladies' fingers
- 1 green chilli, slit
- 1 teaspoon red chilli powder
- 2 kokum rinds
- Salt to taste
- 2 teaspoons coarsely pounded groundnuts

For the tempering

- 2 teaspoons oil
- ½ teaspoon mustard seeds
- ½ teaspoon asafoetida
- ½ teaspoon turmeric powder

- Wash and dry the ladies' fingers well, as they tend to become very sticky.
- For the tempering, heat the oil, add the mustard seeds, asafoetida and turmeric powder.
- Add the green chilli, mix well. Add the ladies' fingers and toss well for 2 minutes on high heat.
- Reduce the heat and add the red chilli powder, kokum rinds, and salt. Cook covered for 3-4 minutes on low heat, till done.
- Add the pounded groundnuts, mix well and serve hot.

Taakaatli Bhendi

- ½ kg ladies' fingers (bhendi)
- ½ vati coarsely pounded groundnuts
- 2 green chillies, slit
- ½ inch ginger
- 2 teaspoons cumin seeds
- 1 vati buttermilk (taak)
- 1 teaspoon sugar
- Salt to taste

For the tempering

2 teaspoons ghee

2 teaspoons cumin seeds

- Wash and dry the ladies' fingers well as they tend to become very sticky. Cut them vertically into medium pieces.
- Grind together pounded groundnuts, green chillies, ginger and cumin seeds. Add this mixture to the buttermilk.
- To the buttermilk mixture, add the ladies' fingers and cook on low heat for 5-6 minutes. Add the sugar and salt. Do not boil the mixture as the butter milk will split.
- For the tempering, heat the ghee and add the cumin seeds. Add the tempering to the ladies' fingers and cook, till done. Serve hot.

Bharlele Bhendi

½ kg ladies' fingers

2 tablespoons coarsely pounded groundnuts

2 tablespoons coarsely pounded sesame seeds

1 teaspoon red chilli powder

1 teaspoon godaa powder

1 teaspoon coriander-cumin powder

Salt to taste

½ teaspoon sugar

2 teaspoons oil

Wash, dry and slit the ladies' fingers vertically in such a way that they can be stuffed with masala.

Mix together the pounded groundnuts, pounded sesame seeds, all the dry masalas, salt and sugar.

Stuff this masala mixture into the ladies' fingers.

Heat the oil and add ladies' fingers one by one and slow roast them on low heat, till done.

If they are too sticky add a kokum rind to them at this stage.

Serve hot.

Ambaadichi Bhaaji

- 1 bunch red sorrel leaves (ambaadi)
- 2 green chillies, slit
- 2 teaspoons gram flour
- ¼ vati split Bengal gram (chana dal)
- ¼ vati groundnuts
- ¼ vati coarsely ground rice (tandul ravaa)
- ½ teaspoon salt
- ½ teaspoon jaggery
- 7-8 garlic cloves
- 2 red chillies
- ¼ vati lime juice (missing in method)

For the tempering

- 2-3 teaspoons oil
- ½ teaspoon mustard seeds
- ½ teaspoon asafoetida
- ½ teaspoon turmeric powder

- Clean and wash the red sorrel and strain.
- Finely chop the red sorrel, and pressure cook with the green chillies, till 1 whistle is released.
- Add the gram flour to the sorrel and mix well to ensure that no lumps are formed.
- To the split Bengal gram, add the groundnuts, coarsely ground rice, salt, jaggery and cooked sorrel, and stir well.
- For the tempering, heat the oil, add the mustard seeds, asafoetida and turmeric powder.
- Add the garlic and red chillies. Add this tempering to the bhaaji and serve hot.

Methichi Bhaaji

- 1 bunch fenugreek leaves (methi)
- 2 green chillies, slit
- ½ vati water
- 2-3 teaspoons gram flour
- ¼ vati groundnuts or fresh green peas
- ½ teaspoon salt
- 1 tablespoon jaggery

For the tempering

- ½ teaspoon oil
- 5-6 garlic cloves, crushed
- 2 red chillies, crushed

Clean, wash and chop the fenugreek leaves.

Cook the fenugreek leaves with and the green chilli and ½ vati of water, on low heat for a couple of minutes.

Remove from heat, add the gram flour and mix well.

Add the groundnuts or fresh peas, salt and jaggery, and cook for 2-3 minutes on the low heat.

For the tempering, heat the oil, add the garlic cloves and red chillies. Add this tempering to the bhaaji and serve hot.

Methichi Moong Dal Bhaaji

- 1 bunch fenugreek leaves (methi)
- ½ vati skinless split green gram (moong dal)
- 2 green chillies, slit
- 1 teaspoon godaa masala
- ½ teaspoon salt
- ½ teaspoon jaggery

For the tempering

- 2 teaspoons oil
- 7-8 garlic cloves, crushed
- 2 red chillies, crushed

Clean, wash and chop the fenugreek leaves. Soak the split green gram for an hour and strain.

To the fenugreek leaves, add the dal and green chillies. Cook on the low heat for a couple of minutes.

Once the split green gram is cooked well add the godaa masala, salt and jaggery.

For the tempering, heat the oil, add the crushed garlic and red chillies.

Add this tempering to the and serve hot.

Methi Batata Bhaaji

- 1 bunch fenugreek leaves (methi)
- 1 medium potato (batata)
- 1 green chilli, chopped
- 1 teaspoon red chilli powder
- ½ teaspoon salt
- ½ teaspoon jaggery

For the tempering

- 2 teaspoons oil
- ½ teaspoon mustard seeds
- ½ teaspoon asafoetida

- Clean, wash and chop the fenugreek leaves. Peel and cut the potato in medium pieces.
- For the tempering, heat the oil, add the mustard seeds and asafoetida.
- Add the green chilli. Add the potato and cook covered for a couple of minutes.
- Add the fenugreek leaves, red chilli powder, salt and jaggery. Cook covered for another 2-3 minutes, till done. Serve hot.

Palak Taakatli Bhaaji

- 1 bunch spinach leaves (palak)
- ½ vati split Bengal gram (chana dal)
- ½ vati groundnuts
- 2 green chillies, chopped
- ½ vati water
- 2 teaspoons gram flour
- 2 vatis sour buttermilk
- ½ teaspoon salt
- ½ teaspoon sugar

For the tempering

- 2 teaspoons oil
- ½ teaspoon mustard seeds
- ½ teaspoon cumin seeds
- ½ teaspoon asafoetida
- ½ teaspoon turmeric powder

- Wash and chop the spinach leaves. Soak the split Bengal gram and groundnuts for an hour.
- To the spinach leaves, add the green chillies and ½ vati water, and cook for a 5 minutes on low heat.
- Add the gram flour and mix well to ensure no lumps are formed. Add the buttermilk and the rest of the ingredients. Cook covered for 5 minutes and just when it begins to boil, take it off the heat.
- For the tempering, heat the oil, add the mustard seeds, cumin seeds, asafoetida and turmeric powder. add the tempering to the bhaaji, mix well and serve hot.

Dal Palak

- 1 bunch spinach leaves (palak)
- ½ vati skinless split green gram (moong dal)
- 2 green chillies, chopped
- 1 kokum rinds
- ½ teaspoon salt
- ½ teaspoon sugar
- ½ vati water

For the tempering

- 1 teaspoon oil
- ½ teaspoon mustard seeds
- ½ teaspoon asafoetida
- 4-5 garlic cloves

Wash and chop the spinach leaves. Soak the split green gram for 30 minutes.

To the spinach leaves, add the split green gram and green chillies. Cook covered for 4-5 minutes on low heat.

Mix well and add the rest of the ingredients and ½ vati of water, if required.

For the tempering, heat the oil, add the mustard seeds, asafoetida and garlic cloves.

Add this tempering to the bhaaji and serve hot.

Palak Bhaaji

- 1 bunch spinach leaves (palak)
- 1 small onion
- 2 green chillies, chopped
- ¼ teaspoon sugar
- ½ teaspoon salt
- 1 medium tomato, chopped
- ¼ vati grated fresh coconut

For the tempering

- 2 teaspoons oil
- ½ teaspoon mustard seeds
- ½ teaspoon asafoetida
- ½ teaspoon turmeric powder

Wash and chop the spinach leaves. Finely chop the onion.

For the tempering, heat the oil, add the mustard seeds, asafoetida and turmeric powder.

Add the onion and chillies, and toss for a couple of minutes. Add the sugar and salt.

Once the onion turn transparent, add the tomato and spinach leaves, cook covered for 45 minutes, till done.

Garnish with grated coconut and serve hot.

Palak–Shepu Bhaaji

- 1 bunch palak leaves (palak)
- 1 bunch dill leaves (shepu)
- ¼ vati split Bengal gram (chana dal) or skinless split green gram (moong dal)
- 3 green chillies, chopped
- 1 medium onion, finely chopped or 5-6 crushed garlic cloves
- ½ teaspoon salt
- ½ teaspoon sugar
- ½ vati grated fresh coconut

For the tempering

- 2 teaspoons oil
- ½ teaspoon mustard seeds
- ½ teaspoon asafoetida

- Wash and finely chop both the vegetables. Soak the split Bengal gram for an hour.
- For the tempering, heat the oil, add the mustard seeds and asafoetida.
- Add the chillies, add either the onion or garlic cloves as per ones liking, and toss till they cook.
- Add the dal and cook covered for 5-6 minutes.
- Add the chopped vegetables and cook for another 5 minutes on low heat, till done. Add the salt and sugar.
- Garnish with grated coconut and serve.

Kardai Golaa Bhaaji

- 1 bunch safflower leaves (kardai)
- 2 green chillies, slit
- 1 vati water
- 2 teaspoons gram flour
- ¼ vati split Bengal gram (chana dal)
- ¼ vati groundnuts
- 1 teaspoon red chilli powder
- 2 kokum rinds
- ½ teaspoon salt
- ½ teaspoon jaggery

For the tempering

- 1 teaspoon oil
- 6-7 crushed garlic cloves

- Wash and chop the safflower leaves.
- Pressure cook the vegetables with the green chillies and about 1 vati water, till 2 whistles are released.
- Once cooked add the gram flour and mix well.
- Add the split Bengal gram, groundnuts and the rest of the ingredients and cook for about 5-6 minutes on low heat, till done.
- For the tempering, heat the oil and add the garlic cloves. Add the tempering to the bhaaji and serve hot.

Tip: *Instead of gram flour, you can use moong dal, and also add ¼ vati coarsely pounded groundnuts to this bhaaji.*

Red/Green Maath Bhaaji

- 1 bunch red amaranth leaves or green amaranth leaves (maath)
- 1 medium onion
- 2 teaspoons oil
- 2 green or red chillies, chopped
- ½ teaspoon salt
- ½ teaspoon sugar
- ¼ vati grated fresh coconut

Tip: *You can also add tomatoes, along with the onion, and use a tempering of ½ teaspoon mustard seeds and asafoetida, each.*

Wash and chop the amaranth. Finely chop the onion.

Heat the oil, add the onion and chillies and toss well, till the onions turn transparent.

Add the amaranth and cook covered for 4-5 minutes on low heat.

Add the salt and sugar and cook, till done.

Garnish with fresh coconut and serve hot.

Mulaa Bhaaji

- 1 bunch radishes (mulaa)
- 2 green chillies, chopped
- ½ vati gram flour
- ½ teaspoon salt
- ½ teaspoon sugar

For the tempering

- 2 teaspoons oil
- ½ teaspoon mustard seeds
- ½ teaspoon asafoetida
- ½ teaspoon turmeric powder

Wash and chop the radishes.

For the tempering, heat the oil, add the mustard seeds, asafoetida and turmeric powder.

Add the green chillies and radishes, and cook covered for 5-6 minutes.

Add the gram flour. Mix well and toss. Cook covered for 5 minutes, till done. Add the salt and sugar, mix well and serve hot.

Tip: *Instead of using gram flour, you can add soaked chana dal or moong dal to the tempering.*

Aluche Phatphate

- 2 bunches colocasia leaves (alu)
- 1 small bunch of green sorrel (small leafy vegetable), if not available tamarind can be used
- 1 white radish
- ¼ vati split Bengal gram
- ¼ vati groundnuts
- ¼ vati cashew nuts
- ½ teaspoon oil
- 2 green chillies, slit
- ½ vati water
- 2 teaspoons gram flour
- 1 teaspoon salt
- Lemon sized tamarind ball
- 2 teaspoons jaggery
- 1 teaspoon red chilli powder
- 1 teaspoon godaa masala
- 1 teaspoon coriander-cumin powder

For the tempering

- 1½ teaspoons oil
- ½ teaspoon mustard seeds
- ½ teaspoon asafoetida
- ½ teaspoon turmeric powder
- ½ teaspoon fenugreek seeds (methi seeds)
- ½ teaspoon cumin seeds

- Wash and chop the colocasia leaves and sorrel leaves finely. Chop the radish into small pieces.
- Soak the split Bengal gram, groundnuts and cashew nuts in water.
- Heat the oil, add the vegetable, green chillies, ½ vatis of water and cook for 5-6 minutes on low heat, till done.
- Adjust the quantity of water, as required.
- Add the gram flour and mix well to ensure no lumps are formed.
- Add all the other ingredients, mix well and cook on low heat for 5-6 minutes, till done.
- For the tempering, heat the oil, add the mustard seeds, asafoetida, turmeric powder, fenugreek seeds and cumin seeds.
- Add the tempering to the bhaaji and serve hot.

Tip: *Green sorrel is called ambat chukaa and is easily available at the vegetable vendor.*

Kaakadichi Upvaas Bhaaji

- 1 big green cucumber (kaakadi)
- 2 teaspoons ghee
- ½ teaspoon cumin seeds
- 2 green chillies
- Salt to taste
- ½ teaspoon sugar
- ¼ vati coarsely pounded groundnuts
- ¼ vati coriander leaves
- ¼ vati grated fresh coconut

Wash and chop the cucumber into medium pieces.

Heat the ghee and add the cumin seeds and green chillies. Add the cucumber and cook covered for 4-5 minutes, till done. Add the salt and sugar.

Add the pounded groundnuts, coriander leaves and grated coconut. Serve hot.

Tips:

This bhaaji is especially prepared for fasting days.

Ladies' fingers can also be prepared the same way.

Batata Upvaas Bhaaji

- ½ kg potatoes (batata)
- 2 teaspoons ghee
- ½ teaspoon cumin seeds
- 2 green chillies
- ¼ vati coarsely pounded groundnuts
- Salt to taste
- ½ teaspoon sugar
- ¼ vati coriander leaves
- ¼ vati grated fresh coconut

Boil, peel and chop the potatoes into small pieces.

Heat the ghee and add cumin seeds, green chillies and toss well.

Add the pounded groundnuts, salt, sugar, coriander leaves and grated coconut, cook for another 2-3 minutes, till done.

Serve hot.

Tip: *The word upvaas means fasting in Marathi.*

Usal and Pithale

These are protein rich and can be enjoyed on days when no fresh vegetables are available. Sprouted usal accompanied with koshimbir is a complete meal in itself, which is not only enjoyable but also very healthy too.

Matki Usal

1 vati sprouted moth beans (matki)

2 green chillies, chopped

Warm water, as required

1 teaspoon coriander-cumin powder

1 teaspoon godaa masala

½ teaspoon red chilli powder

½ teaspoon salt

½ teaspoon jaggery

¼ teaspoon tamarind pulp

¼ vati coriander leaves

¼ vati grated fresh coconut

For the tempering

1 teaspoon oil

½ teaspoon mustard seeds

½ teaspoon asafoetida

½ teaspoon turmeric powder

5-6 curry leaves

Wash the sprouted beans well.

For the tempering, heat the oil, add the mustard seeds, asafoetida, turmeric powder and curry leaves.

Add the green chillies and sprouted beans and mix well.

Add warm water as required, and cook covered on the low heat for 5 minutes.

Add all the dry masalas, jaggery, tamarind pulp and cook on low heat for 5-7 minutes, till done.

Add the coriander leaves and grated coconut, and serve hot.

Tip: *Chawli, moong and masoor usal can be made the same way.*

Kadvyaa Vaal Usal

- 1 vati field beans (vaal/dalimbyaa)
- ¼ vati grated fresh coconut
- ¼ inch ginger
- 2 green chillies
- ½ teaspoon cumin seeds
- 5-6 curry leaves
- 1 vati warm water
- 1 teaspoon coriander-cumin powder
- ½ teaspoon salt
- ½ teaspoon jaggery
- ½ vati coriander leaves

For the tempering

- 1 teaspoon oil
- ½ teaspoon mustard seeds
- ½ teaspoon asafoetida
- ½ teaspoon turmeric powder

- Soak the field beans in the night. Strain the next day and allow them to sprout.
- Then place them it in warm water so that it becomes easy to peel them. The inner seeds are white in colour.
- Grind together the coconut, ginger, green chillies and cumin seeds.
- For the tempering, heat the oil, add the mustard seeds, asafoetida and turmeric powder.
- Add the curry leaves, sprouted beans, and mix well and add 1 vati of warm water and cook covered for 5-6 minutes.
- Add the ground masala, coriander-cumin powder, salt, jaggery and coriander leaves. Simmer for 5-6 minutes, till done. Serve hot.

Kaalaa Vatana Usal

- 1 vati soaked dried black peas (kaalaa vatana)
- 1 small onion
- 8 10 curry leaves
- 1 teaspoon coriander-cumin powder
- 1 teaspoon godaa masala
- 1 teaspoon red chilli powder
- ½ teaspoon jaggery
- ½ teaspoon salt
- Water, as required

For the tempering

- 1 teaspoon oil
- ½ teaspoon mustard seeds
- ½ teaspoon asafoetida
- ½ teaspoon turmeric powder

Soak the black peas at night and strain the next day. Finely chop the onion.

For the tempering, heat the oil in a cooker, add the mustard seeds, asafoetida and turmeric powder.

Add the curry leaves, onion and black peas. Stir well for a minute and then add all the dry masalas, jaggery, salt and water as required.

Pressure cook this mixture till 3 whistles are released, then simmer for 2 minute, till done. Serve hot.

Kulith Usal

- 1 vati horse gram (kulith/hulge)
- 8-10 curry leaves or 8-10 crushed garlic cloves
- 2 red chillies
- ½ teaspoon salt
- ½ teaspoon jaggery
- Warm water, as required

For the tempering

- 2 teaspoons oil
- ½ teaspoon mustard seeds
- ½ teaspoon asafoetida
- ½ teaspoon turmeric powder

Soak the horse gram for 8-10 hours at night and strain the next day.

For the tempering, heat the oil in a cooker, add the mustard seeds, asafoetida and turmeric powder.

Add the curry leaves or garlic cloves, red chillies and horse gram and mix well. Add the jaggery and salt.

Add warm water as required, and pressure cook till 3 whistles are released, and then simmer for 2 minutes on low heat, till done. Serve hot.

Tazyaa Danyaanche Usal

- 1 vati fresh green beans (harbhara or chawli or tur or green dana)
- ¼ vati grated fresh coconut
- 1 inch ginger
- 1 green chilli
- 1 medium tomato
- 1 medium potato
- Warm water, as required
- ½ teaspoon sugar or jaggery
- ½ teaspoon salt
- ¼ vati coriander leaves

For the tempering

- 1 teaspoon oil
- ½ teaspoon mustard seeds
- ½ teaspoon asafoetida
- ½ teaspoon turmeric powder
- ¼ teaspoon cumin seeds
- 5-6 curry leaves

- Wash and clean all the fresh beans.
- Grind together the coconut, ginger, chilli and tomato.
- Chop the potato into medium pieces.
- For the tempering, heat the oil, add the mustard seeds, asafoetida, turmeric powder, cumin seeds and curry leaves.
- Add the beans and potato and mix well, add warm water as per the required.
- Add the ground masala, jaggery or sugar, and salt. Cook covered for 5 minutes on low heat, till done.
- Garnish with the coriander leaves and serve hot.

Matar ani Kaju Usal

- 1 vati fresh wet cashew nuts (kaju)
- 2 green chillies
- 1 vati green peas (matar)
- ½ vati grated fresh coconut
- 1 inch ginger
- ½ teaspoon cumin seeds
- Warm water, as required
- 1 teaspoon salt
- 1 teaspoon sugar
- ½ vati coriander leaves
- ½ vati sweet yoghurt

For the tempering

- 1 teaspoon ghee or oil
- ½ teaspoon mustard seeds
- ½ teaspoon asafoetida
- ½ teaspoon turmeric powder

If the wet cashew nuts are unavailable soak dry ones for 30 minutes in warm water and use.

For the tempering, heat the ghee or oil, add the mustard seeds, asafoetida and turmeric powder.

Add 1 green chilli, peas and cashew nuts; mix well.

Grind together the coconut, ginger, cumin seeds, 1 green chilli.

Add this ground masala to the usal. Add warm water as required.

Add the salt, sugar and coriander leaves. Cook covered on low heat for 5 minutes, till done.

Add the sweet yoghurt and serve hot.

Tip: *If using fresh cashew nuts with skin, soak them in warm water for 30 minutes, then remove the skin and use.*

Tur Fresh Dana Pithale

- ½ vati fresh pigeon peas (tur dana)
- 2 green chillies
- ¼ vati grated fresh coconut
- ¼ inch ginger
- ¼ teaspoon salt
- ¼ teaspoon sugar

For the tempering

- 2 teaspoons oil
- ¼ teaspoon mustard seeds
- ¼ teaspoon asafoetida
- ¼ teaspoon turmeric powder

- Grind together all the ingredients coarsely, except the tempering ingredients.
- For the tempering, heat the oil, add the mustard seeds, asafoetida and turmeric powder.
- Add the ground masala, add water if required, and cook covered low heat for 3-4 minutes, till done. Serve hot.

Tip: *Tur dana are fresh, small, and pea-like green in colour. They are available with vegetable vendors, mainly in winter.*

Pithale

- 1 vati gram flour (besan)
- 2 vatis water
- ½ inch ginger
- 2-3 green chillies
- ¼ teaspoon cumin seeds
- 1 large onion, finely chopped
- 1 teaspoon salt
- ¼ vati coriander leaves

For the tempering

- 2 teaspoons oil
- ½ teaspoon mustard seeds
- ½ teaspoon asafoetida
- 5-6 curry leaves
- ½ teaspoon turmeric powder

- Mix the gram flour with water to make thin paste.
- Coarsely pound the ginger, chilli, cumin seeds together in a mortar and pestle.
- For the tempering, heat the oil, add the mustard seeds, asafoetida, curry leaves and turmeric powder.
- Add the onion and the pounded mixture and mix well. Add the gram flour mixture and water, if required, and salt. Cook covered for 3-4 minutes on low heat, till done.
- Garnish with coriander leaves and serve hot.

Tip: *Pithale tastes best with bhakris.*

Golyaancha Pithale

¼ inch ginger
2-3 green chillies
2-3 garlic cloves (optional)
4-5 curry leaves
2-3 vatis water
1 vati gram flour (besan)
¼ vati coriander leaves
Salt to taste

For the tempering

1 teaspoon oil
½ teaspoon mustard seeds
½ teaspoon asafoetida
½ teaspoon turmeric powder

Coarsely pounded the ginger, green chillies and garlic cloves together in a mortar and pestle.

For the tempering, heat the oil, add the mustard seeds, asafoetida and turmeric powder.

Add the curry leaves. Add water if required, cover and bring to a boil.

Add the gram flour, which will form small lumps that resemble gole (balls) in the boiling water.

Add the salt, mix well and cook covered for 3-4 minutes.

Garnish with coriander leaves and serve hot.

Taakatlaa Pithale

1 vati gram flour (besan)
1 vati water
1 vati buttermilk (taak)
1 medium onion
2-3 green chillies
Salt to taste

For the tempering

2 teaspoons oil
½ teaspoon mustard seeds
½ teaspoon asafoetida
5-6 curry leaves
½ teaspoon turmeric powder

Mix the gram flour with water and buttermilk to make a thin paste.

Finely chop the onion and crush the chillies.

For the tempering, heat the oil, add the mustard seeds, asafoetida, curry leaves and turmeric powder.

Add the chillies and onion, toss well.

Add the gram flour mixture and salt. Cook covered on low heat for 5-6 minutes, till done. Serve hot with bhakri.

Zunkaa

- 1 vati gram flour (besan)
- 1 vati water
- 1 medium onion
- 2-3 garlic crushed cloves
- ¼ inch crushed ginger
- 2-3 red chillies
- ¼ vati coriander leaves
- 1 teaspoon salt

For the tempering

- 2 teaspoons oil
- ½ teaspoon mustard seeds
- ½ teaspoon asafoetida
- ½ teaspoon turmeric powder

- Mix the gram flour and water to make a paste.
- Finely chop the onion.
- For the tempering, heat the oil, add the mustard seeds, asafoetida and turmeric powder.
- Add the garlic, ginger, onion, red chillies and mix well.
- Add the gram flour mixture and salt. Cook covered on low heat till the mixture thickens. This is a thick type of pithale.
- Serve hot with bhakri.

Vaatlyaa Dalicha Pithale

- 1 vati split Bengal gram (chana dal)
- ½ inch crushed ginger
- 2 crushed green chillies
- 2-3 crushed garlic cloves
- Salt to taste
- ¼ vati coriander leaves
- 1 kokum rind (optional)

For the tempering

- 2 teaspoons oil
- ½ teaspoon mustard seeds
- ½ teaspoon asafoetida
- ½ teaspoon turmeric powder

- Soak the split Bengal gram for 4-5 hours. Strain and grind coarsely.
- For the tempering, heat the oil, add the mustard seeds, asafoetida and turmeric powder.
- Add the crushed ginger, green chillies and garlic, mix well.
- Add the ground mixture, salt and water, as required.
- Cook covered for 4-5 minutes on low heat, till done.
- Serve hot.

Kulithacha Pithale

1 vati horse gram (kulith) flour

2 vatis water

2 teaspoons oil

2-3 crushed garlic cloves

2 green chillies or 2-3 red chillies or ½ teaspoon red chilli powder

Salt to taste

1-2 kokum rinds

Mix the horse gram flour with water.

Heat the oil and add the crushed garlic, green chillies or red chillies and mix well.

Add the kulith mixture, water if required, salt and kokum rinds.

Cook covered for 4-5 minutes, till done.

Serve hot with bhakri.

Aamti, Saar and Kadhi

These are different types of curries that make any meal extremely delicious with their aromas and flavours. They are protein rich and when combined with vegetables, add another level of fun and wholesomeness to it. Aamti is especially relished with hot rice and ghee on it. A special aamti, which is delicacy of Marathi cuisine is kaatachi aamti. This is served with puran poli and is a unique combination of sweet and spicy together. Saar is like a soup and can be enjoyed hot or cold. Kadhi is best enjoyed with vegetable khichadi or hot rice, which is a very healthy and tasty combination.

Varan

1 vati split pigeon peas (tur dal)
¼ teaspoon turmeric powder
¼ teaspoon asafoetida
¼ teaspoon salt
¼ teaspoon sugar

Pressure-cook the split pigeon peas with turmeric powder and asafoetida. Churn it well.

Add the salt and sugar.

This is varan. It does not require any tempering.

Serve hot with rice.

Aamti Variation 1

1 vati split pigeon peas (tur dal)
2 green chillies
1 inch crushed ginger
4-5 curry leaves
½ teaspoon salt
Jaggery as per taste
2 kokum rinds
¼ vati coriander leaves

For the tempering

1 teaspoon oil
½ teaspoon mustard seeds
½ teaspoon asafoetida
½ teaspoon turmeric powder
½ teaspoon cumin seeds

Pressure-cook the split pigeon peas and churn well.

For the tempering, heat the oil, add the mustard seeds, asafoetida, turmeric powder and cumin seeds.

Add the green chillies, ginger, curry leaves, and dal. Add water, as required.

Add the salt, jaggery, kokum and coriander leaves and boil well.

Tip: *Moong dal or masoor dal can be made in this way too.*

Aamti Variation 2

- 1 vati split pigeon peas (tur dal)
- 2 kokum rinds
- 1 small piece of jaggery
- ½ teaspoon salt
- ¼ inch crushed ginger
- ¼ vati coriander leaves
- 4-5 curry leaves

For the tempering

- 1 teaspoon oil
- ½ teaspoon mustard seeds
- ½ teaspoon asafoetida
- ½ teaspoon cumin seeds
- ½ teaspoon turmeric powder
- 2 green chillies, chopped

- Pressure-cook the split pigeon peas and churn well.
- Add water as required, kokum, jaggery, salt, ginger, coriander leaves and boil on low heat.
- For the tempering, heat the oil, add the mustard seeds, asafoetida, cumin seeds and turmeric powder.
- Add the tempering to the boiling dal and cover immediately and cook, till done.
- Serve hot.

Bhajyaanchi Aamti

- 1 vati split pigeon peas (tur dal)
- 1 vati vegetable, cut into medium pieces (like brinjal, drumstick, or bottle gourd)
- 2 green chillies, chopped
- 4-5 curry leaves
- 1 teaspoon tamarind pulp
- 2 teaspoons jaggery
- ½ teaspoon salt
- ½ vati coriander leaves

For the tempering

- 1 teaspoon oil
- ½ teaspoon mustard seeds
- ½ teaspoon asafoetida
- ½ teaspoon turmeric powder

Pressure-cook the split pigeon peas and churn well.

For the tempering, heat the oil, add the mustard seeds, asafoetida and turmeric powder. Add the green chillies and curry leaves.

Add the vegetable, tamarind pulp, jaggery, salt, coriander leaves and boil the aamti on low heat, till done. Serve hot.

Tip: *You can replace the vegetable with onions that are chopped into medium-sized pieces.*

Panch Dalinchi Aamti

- 1 vati split pigeon peas (tur dal)
- ¼ vati split red lentils (masoor dal)
- ¼ vati skinless split green gram (moong dal)
- ¼ vati split Bengal gram (chana dal)
- ¼ vati skinless split black gram (udid dal)
- 2 green chillies
- ½ teaspoon fenugreek seeds (methi seeds)
- ½ teaspoon turmeric powder
- 5-6 curry leaves
- 5-6 crushed garlic cloves
- ½ teaspoon garam masala
- ½ teaspoon godaa masala
- ½ teaspoon coriander-cumin powder
- ½ teaspoon chilli powder
- ½ teaspoon jaggery
- ½ teaspoon tamarind pulp
- 1 teaspoon salt

For the tempering

- 1 teaspoon oil
- ½ teaspoon mustard seeds
- ½ teaspoon asafoetida
- ½ teaspoon turmeric powder

- Pressure cook all the dals with 1 green chilli, fenugreek seeds, turmeric powder and churn well.
- For the tempering, heat the oil, add the mustard seeds, asafoetida and turmeric powder.
- Add the green chilli, curry leaves and crushed garlic.
- Add the dal and add water as required.
- Add all the dry masalas, jaggery, tamarind pulp, salt and simmer on low heat, till done.
- Serve hot.

Kataachi Aamti

- 1 vati split Bengal gram (chana dal)
- ¾ vati water
- 1 lemon sized tamarind, pulped
- 2-3 teaspoons jaggery
- ¼ teaspoon red chilli powder
- 1 teaspoon godaa masala
- ½ teaspoon coriander-cumin powder
- ½ teaspoon turmeric powder
- 5-6 curry leaves
- ½ teaspoon salt

For the tempering

- 1 teaspoon oil
- ½ teaspoon mustard seeds
- ½ teaspoon asafoetida
- ½ teaspoon turmeric powder
- 3-4 crushed garlic cloves (optional)

Kataacha masala

- 2 black peppercorns
- 1 clove
- ½ inch cinnamon
- ¼ teaspoon cumin seeds
- ½ vati grated dry coconut

Dry-roast the kataacha masala ingredients and pound them with a mortar and pestle or grind them coarsely in a mixer.

Boil the split Bengal gram in ¾ vati water. Strain and retain all the water.

To this water add the rest of the ingredients, including the katacha masala, and cook on low heat till it boils.

For the tempering, heat the oil, add the mustard seeds, asafoetida and turmeric powder.

Add the tempering to the aamti and cook covered, till done.

Serve hot with puran poli and fresh ghee.

Tips:

You can grind split Bengal gram with jaggery to make the stuffing for puran poli.

This aamti is a speciality dish made with puran poli.

Kulithacha Kat

- 1 vati horse gram (kulith/hulge)
- 3-4 vatis water
- 2 vatis buttermilk
- ½ teaspoon salt
- ¼ teaspoon turmeric powder
- ½ teaspoon sugar
- ¼ vati coriander leaves

For the tempering

- 1 teaspoon ghee
- ¼ teaspoon cumin seeds

- Soak the horse gram for 5-6 hours and pressure cook them with 3-4 vatis of water, till 3 whistles are released.
- Strain the horse gram and retain the water.
- To this water add the buttermilk, salt, turmeric powder, sugar and simmer it on the low heat. Add the coriander leaves.
- For the tempering, heat the ghee and add the cumin seeds.
- Add the tempering to the horse gram. Serve hot.

Tip: *Kulith can be used to make usal.*

Kaalya Vatanachi Aamti

- 1 vati black peas (kaala vatana)
- ½ vati grated dry coconut
- ½ teaspoon cumin seeds
- 2 teaspoons godaa masala
- 1 teaspoon coriander-cumin powder
- 1 teaspoon red chilli powder
- ½ teaspoon salt
- ½ teaspoon turmeric powder
- 1 teaspoon jaggery
- 4-5 curry leaves

For the tempering

- 1 teaspoon oil
- ½ teaspoon mustard seeds
- ½ teaspoon asafoetida
- ½ teaspoon cumin seeds

Soak the black peas for 5-6 hours and then pressure cook till 3 whistles are released.

Roast the dry coconut and cumin seeds for 2 minutes and grind coarsely.

For the tempering, heat the oil, add the mustard seeds, asafoetida and cumin seeds.

Add the cooked peas, ground masala and all the other ingredients, and allow it to boil for 3-4 minute on low heat, till done. Serve hot.

Goda Vaalaachi Aamti

- 1 vati field beans (goda vaal)
- 2 green chillies
- 2 vatis water
- ¼ vati grated fresh coconut
- ¼ teaspoon cumin seeds
- 4-5 curry leaves
- 1 teaspoon tamarind pulp
- 2 teaspoons jaggery
- 1½ teaspoons coriander-cumin powder
- ½ teaspoon red chilli powder
- ½ teaspoon salt
- ¼ vati coriander leaves

For the tempering

- 1 teaspoon oil
- ½ teaspoon mustard seeds
- ½ teaspoon cumin seeds
- ½ teaspoon asafoetida
- ¼ teaspoon turmeric powder

- Wash the field beans well.
- Add 1 green chilli to the beans and boil the beans in 2 vatis of water.
- Grind together the grated coconut, 1 green chilli and cumin seeds.
- For the tempering, heat the oil, add the mustard seeds, cumin seeds, asafoetida and turmeric powder.
- Add the curry leaves and add cooked beans.
- Add the ground masala and all the other ingredients, and simmer on low heat, till done.
- Garnish with coriander leaves and serve hot.

Masoor Aamti

- 1 vati split red lentils (masoor)
- 4 vatis water
- ½ vati grated dry coconut
- ¼ teaspoon cumin seeds
- 2 red chillies
- ¼ inch crushed ginger
- 2 kokum rinds or 1 teaspoon tamarind pulp
- 2 teaspoons jaggery
- ½ teaspoon salt
- ¼ vati coriander leaves

For the tempering

- 1 teaspoon oil
- ½ teaspoon mustard seeds
- ½ teaspoon cumin seeds
- ½ teaspoon asafoetida
- ½ teaspoon turmeric powder

Dry-roast the lentils for 2-3 minutes on low heat, till they turns slight red. Boil the lentils in 4 vatis of water.

Dry-roast the coconut, cumin seeds, red chillies and grind them together.

For the tempering, heat the oil, add the mustard seeds, cumin seeds, asafoetida and turmeric powder. Add the cooked lentils along with the water it was boiled in.

Add the ground masala, crushed ginger, tamarind pulp, jaggery and salt, simmer on low heat, till done.

Garnish with coriander leaves and serve hot.

Tip: *Green moong and chowli aamti can be prepared the same way.*

Moda Kaddhanya Aamti

- 1 vati sprouted red lentils (masoor) or green gram (moong) or sprouted moth beans (matki) or sprouted black eyed peas (chawli) or garbanzo beans (chole/chickpeas)
- 4-5 curry leaves
- ½ vati grated fresh coconut
- 2 red chillies
- 1 inch ginger
- ¼ teaspoon cumin seeds
- 2 kokum rinds or 1½ teaspoons tamarind pulp
- 2 teaspoons jaggery
- ½ teaspoon salt
- ¼ vati coriander leaves

For the tempering

- 1 teaspoon oil
- ½ teaspoon mustard seeds
- ½ teaspoon asafoetida
- ½ teaspoon turmeric powder
- 1 slit green chilli

- For the tempering, heat the oil, add the mustard seeds, asafoetida, turmeric powder and green chilli.
- Add the curry leaves and sprouts of your choice.
- Grind together the fresh coconut, red chillies, ginger and cumin seeds. Add water as required, and the ground masala.
- Add the tamarind or kokum rinds, jaggery, salt, simmer on low heat for 5-6 minutes, till done.
- Garnish with the coriander leaves and serve hot.

Patwadichi Aamti

For the patwadi

- 1 vati gram flour (besan)
- ½ teaspoon salt
- ½ vati buttermilk
- ½ vati water
- ½ teaspoon coarsely pounded ginger and green chillies

For the tempering

- 1 teaspoon oil
- ¼ teaspoon mustard seeds
- ¼ teaspoon asafoetida
- ¼ teaspoon turmeric powder

For the aamti

- ¼ vati grated dry coconut
- ¼ inch ginger
- 2 green chillies
- 2-3 vatis water
- 1½ teaspoons tamarind
- 2 teaspoons jaggery
- ½ teaspoon salt
- ¼ vati coriander leaves

For the tempering

- 1 teaspoon oil
- 1 teaspoon mustard seeds
- 1 teaspoon asafoetida
- 1 teaspoon cumin seeds
- ¼ teaspoon turmeric powder

For the patwadi, mix together the gram flour, salt, pounded chilli and ginger, salt, buttermilk and water, to make a paste.

For the tempering, heat the oil, add the mustard seeds, asafoetida and turmeric powder.

Add the gram flour mixture and stir well as it thickens.

Brush a thali with oil and spread this thickened mixture in it. Allow it to cool and cut into square pieces. These are called patwadi.

For the aamti, grind together the dry coconut, ginger and green chillies.

For the tempering, heat the oil, add the mustard seeds, asafoetida, cumin seeds and turmeric powder.

Add 3 vatis of water, the ground masala, tamarind, jaggery, salt and simmer on low heat, for about 2-3 minutes. Add the patwadi one at a time. As they cook in the aamti they will start floating.

Garnish with coriander leaves and serve hot.

Tip: *Patwadi can also be consumed as a snack, just garnish them with grated fresh coconut and coriander leaves.*

Shengdana Aamti

- ½ vati coarsely pounded groundnuts
- ½ vati buttermilk
- 1 green chilli
- ½ inch ginger
- ½ vati water
- ½ teaspoon salt
- ½ teaspoon sugar
- ¼ vati coriander leaves

For the tempering

- 1 teaspoon ghee
- ½ teaspoon cumin seeds
- 1 green chilli

- Grind together the pounded groundnuts, buttermilk, 1 green chilli and ginger finely. Add water to the mixture.
- To the ground mixture, add the salt and sugar and simmer, on low heat for 3-4 minutes.
- For the tempering, heat the ghee, add the cumin seeds and green chilli. Add the tempering to the aamti and cook covered, till done.
- Garnish with coriander leaves and serve hot.

Tomato Saar

- ½ kg ripe red tomatoes
- ½ vati grated fresh coconut
- 4-5 black peppercorns
- ½ teaspoon salt
- ½ teaspoon sugar

For the tempering

- 1 teaspoon ghee
- ¼ teaspoon cumin seeds

- Wash and boil the tomatoes for 10 minutes.
- Strain, peel and cool them.
- Grind the tomatoes and strain the juice.
- Grind together the coconut, black peppercorns, salt and sugar.
- Add the tomato juice to the ground masala and simmer on low heat for 7-8 minutes.
- For the tempering, heat the ghee and add the cumin seeds. Add the tempering to the saar and cook covered, till done.
- Serve it hot.

Taakaachi Kadhi

- ½ teaspoon cumin seeds
- ½ inch ginger
- 2 green chillies
- 2 vatis sour buttermilk (taak)
- 1 vati water
- 2 teaspoons gram flour (besan)
- ½ teaspoon sugar
- ½ teaspoon salt
- ¼ vati coriander leaves

For the tempering

- 1 teaspoon ghee
- 1 teaspoon mustard seeds
- 1 teaspoon cumin seeds
- 1 teaspoon asafoetida
- 1 teaspoon turmeric powder
- 4-5 curry leaves

Coarsely pound the cumin seeds, ginger, green chillies in a mortar and pestle.

Add the pounded mixture to the buttermilk. Add water if required.

Add the gram flour and churn well to ensure no lumps are formed.

Add the sugar and salt, and simmer on low heat for 7-8 minutes.

For the tempering, heat the ghee and add the mustard seeds, cumin seeds, asafoetida, turmeric powder and curry leaves.

Add the tempering to the kadhi, cover and let it simmer for 30 seconds.

Garnish with coriander leaves and serve hot.

Tip: *You can also add 4-5 crushed garlic cloves to the tempering. Vegetables like cucumber, bottle gourd or colocasia root can be added, while simmering, to enrich the flavour of the kadhi.*

Golyaanchi Kadhi

For the gole (balls)

- 1 vati split Bengal gram (besan)
- ¼ inch ginger
- ¼ teaspoon cumin seeds
- 2 green chillies
- ½ teaspoon salt
- ½ teaspoon sugar
- 2 pinches asafoetida

For the tempering

- 1 teaspoon oil
- 1 teaspoon mustard seeds
- 4-5 red chillies, chopped

- For the kadhi, follow the same method as Takaachi Kadhi till the kadhi is simmering.
- For the gole, soak the split Bengal gram for 3-4 hours and strain it till dry.
- Add the rest of the ingredients and grind coarsely. Prepare small gole (balls) with the mixture.
- Once the kadhi is simmering add the gole one at a time into it. As they cook they will float in the kadhi.
- For the tempering, heat the oil, add mustard seeds and 4-5 red chillies.
- Break the gole and pour this tempering over them.
- Serve hot.

Bhaat

Rice is the staple food of the Konkan Brahmins and is an integral component of the main meal. A variety of rice recipes are shared throughout this book and can be enjoyed as a complete meal in itself. Remember to always soak the rice in advance before cooking as it cooks and tastes better.

Saada Bhaat

- 1 vati rice (tandul)
- 2 vatis water
- ¼ teaspoon ghee
- ½ teaspoon salt

- Clean and wash the rice.
- Add the water to the rice and place on heat.
- Once it boils add the salt and ghee and cook, till done.
- Serve hot.

Jeera Bhaat

- 1 vati rice (tandul)
- ½ teaspoon ghee
- ¼ teaspoon cumin seeds (jeera)
- 2 vatis hot water
- ¼ teaspoon salt

- Clean and wash the rice.
- Heat the ghee, add the cumin seeds and rice, and stir for a couple of minutes.
- Add the hot water and salt, and cook covered, till done.
- Serve it hot.

Kairi Bhaat

- 1 vati rice (tandul)
- ¼ vati grated fresh coconut
- ¼ teaspoon cumin seeds
- ½ teaspoon red chilli powder
- Salt to taste
- ½ vati raw mango (kairi)

For the tempering

- 2-3 teaspoons ghee
- ½ teaspoon cumin seeds
- 1 teaspoon split Bengal gram (chana dal)
- 1 teaspoon skinless split black gram (udid dal)
- 2 red chillies
- 5-6 curry leaves

Clean and wash the rice.

Cook the rice till almost done, so that each grain is separate.

Grind together the coconut and cumin seeds.

Mix the rice with the red chilli powder, salt and ground masala.

For the tempering, heat the ghee, add the cumin seeds, split Bengal gram, skinless split black gram, red chillies and curry leaves.

Add the rice and stir for 2-3 minutes and cook covered for a couple of minutes, till done. Serve hot.

Masala Khichadi

- 1 vati rice (tandul)
- 1 vati skinless split green gram (moong dal)
- 2 green chillies
- 4-5 curry leaves
- ¼ vati grated fresh coconut
- ½ teaspoon cumin seeds
- ¼ vati cut vegetables (such as carrot, bottle gourd, French beans, potato, cauliflower)
- ½ teaspoon salt
- 3 vatis hot water
- ½ vati coriander leaves

For the tempering

- 1 teaspoon oil
- ¼ teaspoon mustard seeds
- ¼ teaspoon asafoetida
- ¼ teaspoon cumin seeds
- ¼ teaspoon turmeric powder

- Clean and wash the rice and split green gram.
- For the tempering, heat the oil, add the mustard seeds, asafoetida, cumin seeds and turmeric powder.
- Add 1 slit green chilli, curry leaves, split green gram and rice, and toss well for a couple of minutes.
- Add the vegetables and salt and mix well.
- Grind together the coconut, 1 green chilli and cumin seeds finely.
- To the rice, add the ground masala and hot water, and cook covered, till done.
- Garnish with the coriander leaves. Serve hot with ghee.

Tip: *This can be prepared in a pressure cooker with just 2 whistles.*

Saadhi Khichadi

- 1 vati rice (tandul)
- ½ vati skinless split green gram (moong dal)
- 1 slit green chilli
- ¼ teaspoon salt
- 2½ vatis water

For the tempering

- 1 teaspoon ghee
- ¼ teaspoon cumin seeds
- ¼ teaspoon turmeric powder

Clean and wash the rice and split green gram together.

In a vessel or pressure cooker, for the tempering, heat the ghee, add the cumin seeds and turmeric powder.

Add the green chilli, skinless split green gram, rice, salt and water. Cook covered, till done. Serve hot with ghee.

Tip: *Split green gram can also be used for this recipe too.*

Dahi Bhaat

- 1 vati cooked rice (tandul)
- 1 vati milk
- 1 vati home-made yoghurt (dahi)
- 1 crushed chilli
- ¼ inch crushed ginger
- Sugar to taste
- Salt to taste

For the tempering

- 1 teaspoon ghee
- ¼ teaspoon cumin seeds
- 4-5 curry leaves

To the cooked rice, add the milk and yoghurt.

Add the chilli, ginger, sugar and salt, and mix it well.

For the tempering, heat the ghee, add the cumin seeds and curry leaves.

Add the tempering to the rice and cover it. Mix well and add more yoghurt, if desired. Serve.

Tip: *This rice can be served at room temperature or it can be refrigerated and served cold.*

Masala Bhaat

- 1 vati rice (tandul)
- ½ vati grated fresh coconut
- 1 inch ginger
- ¼ teaspoon cumin seeds
- 2 green chillies
- 8-10 curry leaves
- 1 vati vegetable (see tip)
- 2 teaspoons godaa masala
- 2 teaspoons coriander-cumin powder
- 1 teaspoon red chilli powder
- ½ teaspoon turmeric powder
- ¼ vati fresh yoghurt
- ½ teaspoon jaggery
- ½ teaspoon salt
- 2½ vatis boiled water
- ¼ vati coriander leaves
- ½ vati grated fresh coconut

For the tempering

- 2 teaspoons oil
- ¼ teaspoon mustard seeds
- ¼ teaspoon cumin seeds
- ¼ teaspoon asafoetida

- Clean and wash the rice well. Soak for a couple hours and strain.
- Grind together the coconut, ginger, cumin seeds and chilli coarsely.
- For the tempering, heat the oil, add the mustard seeds, cumin seeds and asafoetida.
- Add the curry leaves and vegetable, and then the rice. Mix well and add the ground masala and all the dry masalas. Mix well and add the yoghurt, jaggery and salt.
- Add the boiled water and cook covered, till done.
- Garnish with coriander leaves and fresh coconut and serve hot.

Tips:

- *You can use vegetables like ivy gourd, cauliflower, carrot, fresh peas in combination or individually.*
- *This rice is a speciality dish made and served at Maharashtrian weddings.*

Naarali Bhaat

1 vati Basmati or Ambemohar rice (tandul)

4 teaspoons ghee

4 cloves

4 small cardamoms

1½ vatis grated fresh coconut (naaral)

½ teaspoon nutmeg powder

¼ vati cashew nut pieces

½ vati sugar

1 vati grated jaggery

A pinch of salt

2 vatis water

Clean, wash and soak the rice for 2 hours and strain.

Heat 3½ teaspoons ghee, and fry the cloves and cardamoms. Add 1 vati grated coconut. Stir well till it turns pinkish in colour. Then add the rice and stir for a couple of minutes.

Add the nutmeg powder, cashew nuts, the remaining coconut, sugar, jaggery, salt and stir till the jaggery melts into the mixture.

Add ½ teaspoon of ghee and water and cook covered, till done.

Kesari Bhaat

1 vati Basmati or Ambemohar rice (tandul)

¼ teaspoon saffron strands (kesar)

2 teaspoons warm milk

4 teaspoons ghee

4 cloves

4 cardamoms

2 vatis boiled water

1½ vatis sugar

Salt to taste

¼ vati cashew nut pieces + brown raisins

Clean, wash and soak the rice for 2 hours and strain.

Soak the saffron in the warm milk and allow it to dissolve well.

Heat the ghee and fry the cloves and cardamoms.

Add the rice and mix well till the rice changes colour.

Add the boiled water and allow it to cook till each grain can be separated, but do not overcook.

Transfer the cooked rice onto a plate and then add the sugar, salt and saffron milk, and mix well. If required, add yellow food colour to enhance the colour of the rice.

Garnish with ghee and serve.

Vari Tandul Khichadi

- ½ vati samo seeds (vari tandul)
- 1 small potato
- ¼ vati coarsely pounded groundnuts
- Salt to taste
- 1 vati water
- 2 tablespoons coriander leaves

For the tempering

- 2 teaspoons ghee
- 2 slit green chillies
- ½ teaspoons cumin seeds

- Clean and wash the samo seeds well. Peel and cut the potato in small pieces.
- For the tempering, heat the ghee, add the green chillies and cumin seeds.
- Add the potato, coarsely pounded groundnuts, salt and samo seeds, and mix well.
- Add the water and cook covered, till done.
- Garnish with the coriander leaves and serve hot.

Tip: *This dish can be cooked without the potato as well.*

Poli, Puri and Paratha

Another very important and tasty component of the principal meal. A hot poli with fresh ghee and jaggery melted on top and then rolled up, is a nostalgic memory for all who have tasted it. Paratha along with a yummy pickle can be a meal by itself or had as breakfast. It is also a great idea for a snack while travelling.

Poli

- 1 vati wholewheat flour (kanik) + for dusting
- Pinch of salt
- Water as required

- To the wholewheat flour, add a pinch of salt and water, as required, and knead to make a soft dough. Keep it covered for 30 minutes and then shape into small balls.
- Sprinkle wholewheat flour on a circular pastry board (polpaat) and roll out the dough ball into a disc (poli) with a rolling pin (latanaa).
- Heat a tawa, and roast the poli on both the sides.
- Serve hot.

Tips:

- *You can apply ghee to the hot poli before serving.*
- *You can also use wholewheat flour, instead of rice flour, for dusting.*
- *When one side is roasted on the tawa, you can roast the other side directly over the flame with a pair of tongs.*
- *When you knead the wholewheat flour with milk and water, it is called dashmi, which is softer.*

Tikhat Mithachi Puri

1 vati wholewheat flour (kanik)
¼ teaspoon turmeric powder
¼ teaspoon carom seeds
¼ teaspoon cumin seeds
1 teaspoon red chilli powder
Salt to taste
1 teaspoon oil + for deep-frying
Water, as required

To the flour, add all the ingredients and water, as required, and knead to make a soft dough.

Shape the dough into small balls and, on a polpaat, roll out the dough balls with a rolling pin, into small puris.

Heat the oil and fry them one at a time. Strain the oil and serve hot.

Palak Puri

1 bunch spinach (palak)
½ inch ginger
4-5 garlic cloves
2 green chillies
Salt to taste
¼ teaspoon pepper powder
Wholewheat flour, as required
Oil for frying + as required

Tips:

While kneading the dough, add 1 tablespoon gram flour to the wheat flour to make the puris more nutritious and tasty.

You can also replace spinach with fenugreek leaves.

Wash, dry and tear the spinach leaves into pieces and grind them.

Grind together the ginger, garlic and green chillies, into a coarse mixture.

Add the ground mixture and salt, to the spinach. Add the pepper powder.

Add the flour and oil, as required, to the spinach mixture and knead to make a soft dough. Cover for 15 minutes and then shape into small balls. With a rolling pin, roll out the dough balls into puris on a polpaat. If required use some flour for dusting the puris.

Heat a tawa, and cook the puris on both the sides with oil.

Serve hot.

Paakatli Puri

- ½ vati refined flour
- ½ vati very fine semolina
- Salt to taste
- ½ vati yoghurt
- 1 vati sugar (saakhar)
- Water, as required
- ½ teaspoon lime juice
- Oil for deep-frying

Tip: *You can add ½ teaspoon saffron strands to the sugar syrup for flavour and colour.*

- To the refined flour, add the semolina, salt and yoghurt, and knead to make a firm dough. Keep the dough covered for an hour.
- Heat the sugar and add adequate water to immerse the sugar completely.
- Add the lime juice and simmer on low heat, till the sugar dissolves to form a single thread consistency syrup.
- Knead the dough well again, and shape into small balls. With a rolling pin, roll them out into puris.
- Heat the oil, deep-fry the puris, and add them to the hot sugar syrup immediately. Allow them to soak in sugar syrup for a couple of minutes.

Matri

- 1 vati refined flour (maida)
- ¼ teaspoon cumin seeds
- 2-3 green chillies, finely chopped
- ¼ teaspoon carom seeds
- Salt to taste
- Water as required
- Oil as required + for deep-frying

- To the refined flour, add the cumin seeds, chillies, carom seeds and salt, water and oil as required, and knead to make a firm dough. Keep the dough covered for 30 minutes and shape into balls.
- Roll them out into round discs and prick them with fork so that they don't puff up while frying.
- Heat the oil and deep-fry the matri. Once cooled, these can be stored in a tight lid jar and served as a snack tea time.

Flower Paratha

1 vati cauliflower florets (phulkobi)

1 vati wholewheat flour (kanik)

1 teaspoon coarse ginger green chilli paste

Juice of ½ a lime

Salt to taste

¼ vati coriander leaves

Oil or ghee, as required

Wash and steam the cauliflower florets.

To the cauliflower, add the wholewheat flour, ginger-chilli paste, lime juice, salt, coriander leaves, water and oil as required, and knead to make a soft dough. Shape the dough into balls and roll them out into round parathas on a polpaat with a rolling pin.

Heat a tawa, and roast the parathas on both the sides with oil or ghee.

Serve hot with chutney.

Methi Paratha

1 bunch fenugreek leaves (methi)

2 teaspoons gram flour (besan)

1 vati wholewheat flour

½ teaspoon coarse ginger-green chilli paste

Salt to taste

Water, as required

Oil or ghee, as required

Wash and chop the fenugreek leaves.

Add the gram flour, wheat flour, ginger-chilli paste, salt, water and oil as required, and knead to make a soft dough. Cover for 15-20 minutes.

Shape the dough into balls and roll them out into round parathas on a polpaat with a rolling pin.

Heat a tawa, and roast the parathas on both the sides with ghee or oil.

Serve hot with chutney.

Kobi Paratha

- 1 vati shredded cabbage (kobi)
- 1 vati wholewheat flour (kanik)
- ½ vati gram flour
- ½ vati very fine semolina
- ½ teaspoon coarse ginger-green chilli paste
- Salt to taste
- ¼ vati coriander leaves (optional)
- Oil or ghee, as required

- To the cabbage, add the wheat flour, gram flour, semolina, ginger-green chilli paste, salt and coriander leaves, water and oil as required, and knead to make a soft dough.
- Keep the dough covered for 15-20 minutes.
- Shape the dough into balls and roll them out into round parathas on a polpaat with a rolling pin.
- Heat a tawa, and roast the parathas on both the sides with oil or ghee.
- Serve hot with chutney.

Mulaayacha Paratha

- 1 vati grated radish with finely chopped greens (mulaa)
- 1 vati wholewheat flour
- 1 vati gram flour
- ½ vati very fine semolina
- 1 teaspoon coarse ginger-green chilli paste
- Salt to taste
- 1 onion, finely chopped
- Water, as required
- Oil or ghee, as required

- To the radish, add the wheat flour, gram flour, semolina, ginger-green chilli paste, salt, onion, water and oil as required, and knead to make a soft dough. Keep the dough covered for 15-20 minutes.
- Shape the dough into balls and roll them out into round parathas on a polpaat with a rolling pin.
- Heat a tawa, and roast the parathas on both the sides with oil or ghee.
- Serve hot with chutney.

Bhakri

1 vati bhakri flour + for dusting

Salt to taste

Warm water, as required

To the bhakri flour, add the salt add warm water, and knead to make a soft dough.

Shape the dough into balls and flatten them with your palms or, dust the polpaat with some dry flour and roll them out into round bhakris, either with your palms or with a rolling pin.

Heat a bhakri tawa, place the bhakri on the tawa and spread a little water over it, then flip it over and roast well.

Serve hot.

Tip: *You can make bhakris with rice flour, sorghum (jowar) flour, millet (bajra) flour, finger millet (nachni) flour or, all of these flours can be mixed together and used as well.*

Pakwaane

These are unique delicacies which are enjoyed during various festivals. Puran poli is made on holidays and gul poli is made during Sankranti. And of course, no Ganesh pujan can be done without ukadiche modak. Olyaa naaralachi karanji is another special delicacy made during Diwali. No meal is complete without these pakwaane.

Puran Poli

For the puran (stuffing)

- 2 vatis split Bengal gram (chana dal)
- 1 teaspoon oil
- 6 vatis water
- 1 vati finely grated jaggery (gul)
- 1 vati sugar
- 1 nutmeg, grated into a fine powder
- ¼ teaspoon salt

For the paari (outside covering)

- 2 teaspoons semolina
- 1 vati wholewheat flour (kanik)
- ½ teaspoon salt
- ½ vati refined flour + for dusting
- 1 vati oil
- Ghee, as required

Tip:

This is a speciality dish made for Holi.

For the puran, wash the split Bengal gram and strain. Add the oil and water. Place on heat, and cook, till done. Strain and retain the water to make kataachi aamti.

To the dal, add the jaggery, sugar, nutmeg powder, salt and cook on low heat, stirring continuously till the mixture starts leaving the sides of the pan.

Add the mixture to a puran maker (or food processor) and churn it, till it becomes very soft. Shape the soft puran into small balls. Rinse the puran maker with water and use this water for kaatachi aamti.

For the paari (outer covering), soak the semolina in a little water.

To the wholewheat flour, add the refined flour, salt and semolina and knead to make a very soft dough. Pour the oil over it and cover it for 4-5 hours.

To make the poli, knead the dough well in the oil and shape the dough into balls.

With your fingers, mould each dough ball into the shape of a small bowl and place a puran ball in it. Enclose it well by bringing all the edges together to make a ball.

Dust the polpaat with some refined flour, if required, and gently roll them out into round polis with a rolling pin.

Heat a tawa, add some ghee and roast the polis well on both sides. Serve hot with ghee and kaatachi aamti.

Besan Poli

- ½ vati refined flour
- 2 vatis wholewheat flour
- ½ teaspoon salt
- ½ teaspoon hot oil (also called mohan)
- Water, as required
- 1½ vatis ghee + for roasting
- 2 vatis gram flour (besan)
- 2½ vatis powdered sugar
- 2 teaspoons cardamom powder
- Rice flour, for dusting

- For the paari (outer covering), to the refined flour, add the wholewheat flour, salt and hot oil, water as required, and knead to make a semi-soft dough. Keep the dough covered for 4-5 hours.
- For the stuffing, heat the ghee, add the gram flour and roast it on low heat for 7-8 minutes, till fragrant.
- Transfer the gram flour onto a plate and add the powdered sugar and cardamom powder. Mix well and shape into small balls.
- To make the poli, knead the dough well after 4-5 hours and shape the dough into balls.
- With your fingers, mould each dough ball into the shape of small bowl and place a gram flour ball in it. Enclose it well by bringing all the edges together to make a ball.
- Dust the polpaat with some rice flour, if required, and gently roll them out into round polis with a rolling pin.
- Heat a tawa, add some ghee and roast the polis well on both sides.
- Serve hot.

Gul Poli

For the paari (outer covering)

- 2 vatis wholewheat flour (kanik)
- ¼ vati refined flour
- ¼ vati gram flour
- ¼ teaspoon salt
- ¼ vati oil

For the saaran (stuffing)

- ¼ vati finely grated dry coconut
- ½ kg jaggery (gul)
- ¼ vati white sesame seeds
- 2 teaspoons poppy seeds
- 1 teaspoon nutmeg powder
- 4 teaspoons hot oil

For the paari, to the wholewheat flour, add the refined flour, gram flour, salt, and water as required, and knead to make a firm dough.

Add the oil and knead again. Shape the dough into balls.

For the saaran, dry-roast the coconut without oil, and grind it to a powder.

Mix together the coconut powder and all the other ingredients of the saaran and knead into small balls.

To make a single gul poli, you need 2 polis and 1 saaran ball each. Roll out the dough balls into round polis on a polpaat, with a rolling pin.

Spread the saaran ball onto the poli, and then cover it with another poli, and seal gently around the edges, with a spoon.

Heat the pan and roast the poli. Serve hot.

Sanjachyaa Poli

For the saaran (stuffing)

- 1 teaspoon ghee
- 1 vati semolina (ravaa)
- 1¼ vatis jaggery (gul)
- A pinch of nutmeg powder
- 2½ vatis water

For the paari (outer covering)

- 1 vati wholewheat flour (kanik)
- ½ vati refined flour
- Salt to taste
- Ghee, as required

- For the paari, mix together all the paari ingredients and knead to make a soft dough. Cover for 1 hour.
- For the saaran, heat the ghee and add sauté the semolina on low heat till fragrant.
- Add the jaggery nutmeg powder, and water, and stir continuously till the mixture thickens. Allow the mixture to cool, and shape into balls.
- To make the poli, shape the dough into balls. With your fingers, mould the dough ball into the shape of a small bowl and place a saaran ball in it.
- Enclose it well by bringing all the edges together to make a ball and gently roll them out into round polis.
- Heat a tawa, add some ghee and roast the polis well on both sides.

Satorayaa

For the saaran (stuffing)

- 1 vati ghee + as required
- 2 vatis semolina
- 2 teaspoons milk
- ¼ kg khavaa (khoya), broken into pieces
- 1 vati powdered sugar
- 2 teaspoons cardamom powder

For the paari (outer covering)

- 1 vati refined flour (maida)
- ½ vati fine semolina (ravaa)
- ½ teaspoon salt
- ½ vati milk
- ½ vati ghee

For the paari, mix together all the paari ingredients and knead to make a firm dough.

For the saaran, heat the ghee and sauté the semolina on low heat till fragrant.

Add the milk and stir continuously. To this add the khavaa and sauté .

Cool the mixture and the add powdered sugar and cardamom powder.

Knead the mixture well and shape into small balls.

To make the poli, and shape the dough into balls.

With your fingers, mould each dough ball into the shape of a small bowl and place a saaran ball in it.

Enclose it well by bringing all the edges together to make a ball and gently roll them out into round polis.

Heat a tawa, add some ghee and roast the polis well on both sides. Serve hot.

Ukadiche Modak

For the saaran (stuffing)

- ½ teaspoon ghee
- 1½ vatis grated fresh coconut
- ½ vati jaggery
- ¼ vati milk
- ½ teaspoon cardamom grains
- ¼ teaspoon white sesame seeds

For the paari (outer covering)

- 1 vati Basmati or Ambemohar rice flour or ready-made modak flour
- 1 vati water
- 1 teaspoon ghee or homemade white butter
- ¼ teaspoon salt

Tip: *This is a speciality dish served as prasad to Lord Ganesh during the Ganpati festival.*

- For the saaran, heat the ghee and add the coconut, jaggery, milk and stir well. Once the jaggery melts and the mixture becomes dry, add the cardamom and white sesame seeds. Mix well and cool.
- For the paari, boil the water and while it is boiling, add ghee or butter and salt. Add the rice flour, stir continuously for 2-3 minutes so that no lumps are formed. Cook covered for 1-2 minutes.
- Grease your hands with ghee and knead to make a soft dough. Shape the dough into balls. Grease your fingers with ghee, whenever required.
- With your fingers, mould the dough ball into the shape of a small bowl and place enough saaran, about 1-1½ teaspoons, to fill it.
- Pinch the edges together to make pleats, then gather the edges towards the top and pinch then together to make a peak.
- Boil water in a steamer, place a banana leaf or apply ghee on the steamer plate. Place the modaks on the plate and steam for 5 minutes on low heat.
- Serve hot with ghee.

Olyaa Naaralachi Karanji

For the paari (outer covering)

- ¼ vati fine semolina (ravaa)
- 2 teaspoons water
- 1 vati sifted refined flour
- ¼ vati ghee
- ½ teaspoon salt
- ¼ teaspoon sugar
- Oil for deep-frying

For the saaran (stuffing)

- 2 teaspoons ghee
- 4 vatis grated fresh coconut (naaral)
- ½ vati sugar
- ½ vati jaggery
- 1 vati milk
- 1 teaspoon cardamom powder

For the paari, add 2 teaspoons of water to the semolina.

Add the all ingredients for the paari, and knead to make a soft dough. Keep the dough covered for 2 hours.

Shape the dough into small balls.

For the saaran, heat the ghee and add all the saaran ingredients. Sauté till the jaggery melts and the mixture dries up. Cool the mixture.

To make the karanji, roll out the dough balls into puris.

Place a spoonful of the saaran on one half of the puri, fold the other half over it and seal the edges tightly.

Heat the oil and deep-fry.

Serve hot.

Shira

- ½ vati milk
- 1 vati sugar (saakhar)
- 1 vati water
- ½ vati ghee
- 1 vati fine semolina (ravaa)
- ½ vati almond pieces and raisins
- ¼ teaspoon cardamom powder
- ¼ teaspoon saffron soaked in 4 teaspoons milk

- Boil the milk, sugar and water together.
- Heat the ghee and sauté the semolina on low heat till fragrant.
- Add the boiled mixture and cook covered for 2 minutes.
- Add the cardamom powder and saffron milk. Serve hot.

Tip: *Over-ripe bananas can also be added to enhance the taste of the dish.*

Kanik Shira

- ½ vati milk
- ½ vati sugar (saakhar)
- ½ vati water
- ¼ vati ghee
- 1 vati coarse wholewheat flour (kanik)
- ¼ teaspoon cardamom powder
- ¼ vati chopped almonds

- Boil the milk, sugar and water together.
- Heat the ghee and sauté the wholewheat flour on low heat for 2-3 minutes till fragrant.
- Add the boiled mixture and cardamom powder. Cook covered for 1-2 minutes till the mixture thickens.
- Garnish with the almonds and serve hot.

Khandavi

- 1 vati milk
- 1 vatis water
- ¼ vati ghee + for greasing
- 1 vati finely ground rice (tandul ravaa)
- 1 vati jaggery
- 1 teaspoon nutmeg powder
- ¼ vati mixed dry fruits (almond, cashew nuts, raisins)

Boil the milk and water together.

Heat the ghee, and sauté the ground rice for 2-3 minutes on low heat.

Add the boiled mixture, jaggery, and nutmeg powder. Cook covered for 1-2 minutes, till the mixture thickens and leaves the sides of the pan.

Transfer the mixture to a plate greased with ghee, spreading the mixture evenly. Allow it to cool.

Sprinkle the dry fruits on top. Cut into pieces and serve.

Daliya Kheer

- 1 vati broken wheat (daliya)
- ½ teaspoon poppy seeds
- ½ vati grated fresh coconut
- A pinch of nutmeg powder
- 1 vati jaggery
- Milk, as required
- Water, as required

Pressure cook the broken wheat till 3-4 whistles are released.

Mix well to form an even consistency.

Add the poppy seeds, coconut, nutmeg powder, jaggery, milk, water to get the desired consistency, and simmer on low heat for 2-3 minutes. Serve hot.

Shevyaancha Kheer

- 1 teaspoon ghee
- 1 vati vermicelli (shevyaa)
- ¾ litre milk
- ¾ litre sugar
- ½ vati chopped dry fruits or ¼ vati dry fruit powder
- ¼ teaspoon cardamom powder
- ¼ teaspoon saffron strands

- Heat the ghee and roast the vermicelli for 2 minutes on low heat.
- Add the milk and all the other ingredients, and stir well for 3-4 minutes, till done. Do not boil the kheer too much.
- Serve hot.

Tandul Kheer

- 1 vati rice (tandul)
- 2 teaspoons ghee
- ¾ litre milk
- ½ vati sugar
- ¼ teaspoon cardamom powder
- ½ vati chopped dry fruits
- ¼ teaspoon saffron strands

- Wash and soak the rice for an hour, and then grind coarsely.
- Heat the ghee, add the ground rice and stir well for a minute.
- Add the milk, sugar and cardamom powder, and cook for 2-3 minutes on low heat, till done.
- Add the dry fruits and saffron strands. Serve hot.

Dudhi Halwa

- ½ kg bottle gourd (dudhi)
- 2 teaspoons ghee
- ½ vati milk
- 1 vati sugar
- 1 vati khavaa
- ½ teaspoon cardamom powder

- Peel and grate the bottle gourd.
- Heat the ghee, add the bottle gourd and sauté for 1-2 minutes on low heat.
- Add the milk, sugar, khavaa, cardamom powder and simmer for 2-3 minutes, till done. Serve hot.

Nyaahari

The word nyaahari means breakfast or an early meal consumed before one leaves for the day's work. Easy to make and tasty, these recipes are such that they can also be consumed at snack time or tea time.

Kairi Panhe Variation 1

- ½ kg Rajapuri raw mangoes (kairi)
- 2 vatis jaggery
- 1 vati sugar
- 2-3 teaspoons salt
- ½ teaspoon cardamom powder
- ¼ teaspoon saffron strands

Note: *Kairi Panhe is a type of sharbat.*

- Wash and soak the mangoes in warm water for 15-20 minutes.
- Immerse the mangoes completely in water, in a pressure cooker, and cook them till 2 whistles are released.
- Strain and preserve the water in which the mangoes were boiled.
- Allow the mangoes to cool, peel them and extract the pulp within.
- Add the pulp to the water that was used to boil the mangoes.
- Add the rest of the ingredients, except the saffron, and stir well on heat, till all the jaggery and sugar dissolves.
- Strain using a fine strainer. Add the saffron and cool in the refrigerator. Serve cold.

Kairi Panhe Variation 2

- ½ kg Rajapuri raw mangoes (kairi)
- 2 vatis sugar
- 2 teaspoons salt

- Wash, peel and shred the mangoes.
- Grind the mangoes, sugar and salt together to a pulp and store in the refrigerator.
- This pulp can be used to make the panhe as and when required, just add 1 tablespoon of the pulp to 1 glass of water.
- Serve cold.

Limbu Sharbat

- 2 limes (limbu)
- 4 teaspoons sugar
- 1 teaspoon salt
- 2 glasses water
- 1-2 saffron strands (optional)

Wash the limes and squeeze out the juice. Add all the remaining ingredients and stir well.

Cool in the refrigerator.

Serve cold.

Pohe

- 1 vati thick flattened rice (jaade pohe)
- 4-5 curry leaves
- 2-3 green chillies, chopped
- 1 small onion, finely chopped
- 1 small potato, peeled and thinly sliced
- ½ teaspoon salt
- ½ teaspoon sugar
- ½ teaspoon lemon juice
- ¼ vati grated fresh coconut
- ¼ vati coriander leaves

For the tempering

- 2 teaspoons oil
- ½ teaspoon mustard seeds
- ½ teaspoon cumin seeds
- ½ teaspoon asafoetida
- ½ teaspoon turmeric powder

Wash the pohe in a strainer, under running water and allow the water to drain away completely.

For the tempering, heat the oil, add the mustard seeds, cumin seeds, asafoetida and turmeric powder.

Add the green chillies, curry leaves, onion and potato, mix well. Cook covered for 2-3 minutes.

Add the strained pohe and toss well. Add the salt, sugar, and lemon juice. Cook covered for 1 minute.

Garnish with coconut and coriander leaves. Serve hot.

Dadpe Pohe

- 1 vati thin flattened rice (paatal pohe)
- 1 small onion, finely chopped
- 1 green chilli, finely chopped
- ¼ vati coriander leaves, finely chopped
- 1 small tomato, finely chopped
- ½ vati grated fresh coconut
- ½ teaspoon metkoot (available in stores)
- ½ teaspoon mango pickle
- ¼ teaspoon salt
- ¼ teaspoon sugar
- 1 teaspoon lemon juice
- 5-6 curry leaves
- 1 poha papad (available in stores)

For the tempering

- ½ teaspoons oil
- ½ teaspoon mustard seeds
- ½ teaspoon cumin seeds
- ½ teaspoon asafoetida
- ½ teaspoon turmeric powder

- Mix together the flattened rice, onion, chilli, coriander leaves, tomato, grated coconut, metkoot, mango pickle, salt, sugar and lemon juice, preferably with your hands, and cover the mixture for about 15-20 minutes.
- For the tempering, heat the oil, add the mustard seeds, cumin seeds, asafoetida and turmeric powder.
- Add the curry leaves and then add the tempering to the covered mixture.
- Mix well and serve with roasted poha papad.

Tel Pohe

1 vati thin flattened rice (paatal pohe)

1 teaspoon oil

½ teaspoon red chilli powder

½ teaspoon lemon juice

¼ teaspoon salt

¼ teaspoon sugar

Mix together all the ingredients, preferably with your hands.

Keep it covered for 10 minutes and serve.

Dahi Pohe

1 vati thick flattened rice (jaade pohe)

1 vati sweet yoghurt (dahi)

1 green chilli, finely chopped

¼ vati coriander leaves

¼ vati salt

¼ teaspoon sugar

Mix together all the ingredients. Keep it covered for 5 minutes and serve.

Tip: *Sandgi mirchi (stuffed and dried masala mirchi) is available in the market and can be fried, crushed and added to dahi pohe.*

Dudh Pohe

1 vati thick pohe (jaade pohe)

¾ vati milk (dudh)

2 teaspoons sugar

Mix together all the ingredients. Keep it covered for 5 minutes and serve.

Sabudana Khichadi

- 1 vati sago (sabudana)
- ½ vati coarsely pounded groundnuts
- ½ teaspoon sugar
- ½ teaspoon salt
- 2 teaspoons ghee
- ½ teaspoon cumin seeds
- 2 green chillies, chopped
- 1 potato, peeled and sliced or 1 boiled potato, cut into small pieces
- 2 teaspoons milk
- ½ vati grated fresh coconut

- Soak the sago for 5-6 hours till soft.
- Add the pounded groundnuts, sugar, and salt and mix well.
- Heat the ghee, add the cumin seeds, green chillies and potato. Toss well and cook covered for 2-3 minutes.
- Add the sabudana mixture, toss well on low heat, and add the milk.
- Toss while cooking for 2-3 minutes.
- Garnish with grated coconut and serve hot.

Vari Khichadi

- 1 vati samo seeds (vari tandul)
- 2 teaspoons ghee
- ½ teaspoon cumin seeds
- 2 green chillies, chopped
- 1 small potato, sliced
- 2½ vatis water
- ½ teaspoon salt
- ½ teaspoon sugar
- 1 vati coarsely pounded groundnuts
- ¼ vati grated fresh coconut

- Wash the samo seeds in water and strain.
- Heat the ghee, add the cumin seeds, green chillies and potato. Cook covered for 2 minutes.
- Add the samo seeds, water, salt and sugar, and toss well.
- Add the pounded groundnuts.
- Garnish with the coconut and serve hot.

Sanjhaa

- 2 green chillies
- 4-5 curry leaves
- 1 onion, finely chopped
- 1 vati semolina (ravaa)
- 1 vati water
- ½ vati buttermilk
- ½ teaspoon salt
- ½ teaspoon sugar
- ½ vati grated fresh coconut
- ½ vati coriander leaves

For the tempering

- 2 teaspoons oil
- ½ teaspoon mustard seeds
- ½ teaspoon cumin seeds
- ½ teaspoon asafoetida
- ½ teaspoon turmeric powder

For the tempering, heat the oil, add the mustard seeds, cumin seeds, asafoetida and turmeric powder.

Add the green chillies, curry leaves and onion.

Add the semolina and sauté till fragrant.

Boil the water and add it to the semolina. Add the buttermilk, salt and sugar. Cook covered, till done.

Garnish with coconut and coriander leaves and serve.

Tip: *Tomatoes, shredded carrots and green peas can also be added to this dish.*

Note: *This is a unique type of Brahmani upma.*

Thalipeeth

- 1 vati Thalipeeth Bhaajni flour (page 10)
- 1 medium onion, finely chopped
- ¼ vati coriander leaves
- 2 teaspoons red chillies
- ¼ teaspoon salt
- ½ teaspoon oil + as required
- Water, as required

- To the bhaajni flour, add the rest of the ingredients, and water as required, and knead to make a soft dough.
- Place a leaf or butter paper on a chopping board and knead a small round ball with greased hands. Spread it with your fingers to form a disc and make a hole in the centre.
- Heat some oil on a tawa and place the thalipeeth on it. Add some oil to the edges of the thalipeeth and cook covered for a minute.
- Roast well on both sides. Serve hot with white butter or yoghurt.

Upvaas Thalipeeth

- ½ vati Upvaas Bhaajni flour (page 10)
- 1 green chillies, finely chopped
- 2 teaspoons coarsely pounded groundnuts
- Salt to taste
- Oil, as required
- Water, as required

- To the upvaas flour, add the chillies, pounded groundnuts, salt, oil and water as required, and knead to make a soft dough.
- Place a leaf or butter paper on a chopping board and knead a small round ball with greased hands. Spread it with your fingers to form a disc and make a hole in the centre.
- Heat some oil on a tawa and place the thalipeeth on it. Add some oil to the edges of the thalipeeth and cook covered for a minute.
- Roast well on both sides and serve.

Bhaajni Ukad

- 1 small onion
- 1 green chilli, slit
- 5-6 curry leaves
- ½ vati water
- ½ vati buttermilk
- 1 vati Thalipeeth Bhaajni flour (page 10)
- ½ teaspoon sugar
- ½ teaspoon salt

For the tempering

- 1 teaspoon oil
- ½ teaspoon mustard seeds
- ½ teaspoon cumin seeds
- ½ teaspoon asafoetida
- ½ teaspoon turmeric powder

For the tempering, heat the oil, add the mustard seeds, cumin seeds, asafoetida and turmeric powder.

Add the onion, green chilli, curry leaves, water, and buttermilk and simmer on low heat.

Once it begins to boil, add the flour, sugar and salt. Stir well so that no lumps are formed.

Mix well to form a thickened mixture. Cook covered for a couple of minutes, till done.

Serve hot.

Tandulachi Ukad

- 1 green chilli, slit
- 6-8 curry leaves
- ½ inch ginger
- ½ vati sour buttermilk
- ½ vati water
- 1 vati rice flour
- ½ teaspoon sugar
- ½ teaspoon salt

For the tempering

- 2 teaspoons oil
- ½ teaspoon mustard seeds
- ¼ teaspoon cumin seeds
- ½ teaspoon asafoetida
- ½ teaspoon turmeric powder

For the tempering, heat the oil, add the mustard seeds, cumin seeds, asafoetida and turmeric powder.

Add the green chilli, curry leaves, ginger, buttermilk and water, and simmer on low heat.

Once it begins to boil, add the flour, sugar and salt. Stir well so that no lumps are formed.

Mix well to form a thickened mixture and cook covered for a couple of minutes, till done.

Serve hot.

Tandul Shevai

- 1 vati rice flour (tandul)
- 2 vatis water
- Salt to taste
- ½ vati thick coconut milk
- ½ vati jaggery
- A pinch of cardamom powder

- Heat the water and add the salt. Once it boils, add the rice flour, mix well to form a thickened mixture.
- Transfer this thickened mixture into a shevai maker and make the shevai.
- Steam the shevai in a steamer.
- To the coconut milk, add the jaggery, cardamom powder. Stir well.
- Once the ingredients in the coconut milk have dissolved, pour it over the steamed shevai and serve hot.

Ghaavan

- 1 vati ghaavan flour
- 1 onion, chopped
- 2 green chillies, finely chopped
- Salt to taste
- ¼ vati coriander leaves
- 2½ vatis water
- Oil, as required

- To the ghaavan flour, add the onion, chillies, salt, coriander leaves, and water to make a thin batter.
- Apply some oil on a heated pan and spread a ladleful of the batter evenly, cover and then drizzle some oil around it.
- Cook well on both sides and serve hot.

Tips:

- *Ghaavan flour is available in the market.*
- *You can add finely chopped fenugreek leaves and spinach to the ghaavan flour.*

Moong Lentil Dosa

1 vati green gram (hirve moong)

¼ vati rice

¼ vati skinless split black gram (udid dal)

1 teaspoon fenugreek seeds (methi seeds)

¼ teaspoon cumin seeds

½ inch ginger

3-4 red chillies

Salt to taste

Water, as required

Oil, as required

Soak the green gram, rice, skinless split black gram, fenugreek seeds separately for 4-5 hours, strain and then grind then with the cumin seeds, ginger and red chillies, to form a thick batter. Add the salt and water as required.

Apply some oil on a heated pan and spread a ladleful of the batter evenly, cover and then drizzle some oil around it.

Cook well on both sides and serve hot with chutney.

Moong Dal Dosa

1 vati skinless split green gram (moong dal)

1 vati skinless split black gram (udid dal)

3-4 green chillies

½ inch ginger

½ teaspoon cumin seeds

Salt to taste

Water, as required

Oil, as required

Soak the dals for 4-5 hours and strain.

Grind the soaked dals with the chillies, ginger, cumin seeds and salt, to make a dosa batter. Add water as required.

Apply some oil on a heated pan and spread a ladleful of the batter evenly, cover and then drizzle some oil around it.

Cook well on both sides and serve hot with chutney.

Ambolyaa

- 1 vati rice (tandul)
- ½ vati skinless split black gram (udid dal)
- 1 teaspoon fenugreek seeds (methi seeds)
- ¼ vati grated fresh coconut
- ¼ vati thin flattened rice (paatal pohe)
- Salt to taste
- Water, as required
- Oil, as required

- Soak the rice, dal and fenugreek seeds in water separately, for 6-7 hours and strain.
- Grind together with fresh coconut, flattened rice and salt, to make a batter.
- Add water as required. Keep the batter covered and allow it to ferment for 7-8 hours. Once fermented, mix well.
- Apply some oil on a heated pan and spread a ladleful of the batter evenly, then drizzle some oil around it. Cook well on both sides and serve hot with chutney.

Tip: *To make sweet ambolyaa add 1 vati jaggery to the batter. Serve it with ghee and honey.*

Panagi

- Banana leaves, as required
- 1 vati rice (tandul) flour
- 2 teaspoons gram flour (besan)
- ½ teaspoon cumin seeds
- Salt to taste
- ¼ vati coriander leaves
- Water, as required
- Oil, as required

- Wash the banana leaves well. Mix together all the ingredients, except the oil. Add water as required, to make a smooth batter.
- Place a piece of the banana leaf on a heated pan, grease it with oil.
- Spread a ladleful of the batter uniformly on the banana leaf and gently cover it with another piece of banana leaf. Cook covered for 1-2 minutes on low heat. If required, drizzle some oil around the edges.
- Flip it gently so that both sides are cooked. Serve hot.

Patolyaa

1 vati rice (tandul) flour
Salt, as required
1 teaspoon oil
6-7 turmeric leaves
Water, as required
1 vati grated fresh coconut
1 vati jaggery

Mix together the rice flour, salt, oil, and water as required, to make a thick batter.

The saaran or stuffing for the patolyaa is the same as for Ukadiche Modak (page 132).

Wash the turmeric leaves and with a ladle spread the rice batter on the leaf.

Gently place the stuffing on one side of the leaf and cover it with the other side.

Steam in a modak steamer for 5 minutes on low heat. Once done, peel the leaf and serve hot.

Tomato Omelette

1 onion, finely chopped
1 tomato, finely chopped
2 green chillies, finely chopped
¼ vati coriander leaves
¼ teaspoon cumin seeds
1 teaspoon salt
½ vati gram flour (besan)
2 teaspoons fine semolina
1 tablespoons rice flour
Water, as required
Oil, as required

Mix together all the ingredients with water as required, to make a thick batter.

Apply some oil on a heated pan and spread a big spoonful of the batter evenly (the size of a pancake). Drizzle some oil around it and cook covered for 1 minute.

Cook well on both sides and serve hot.

Dhokla

- ¼ kg ready-made dhokla flour
- Water, as required
- 1 teaspoon coarse ginger-green chilli paste (optional)
- Salt to taste
- 1 packet Eno fruit salt
- 2 tablespoons coriander leaves
- 2 tablespoons grated fresh coconut

For the tempering

- ½ teaspoon oil
- ½ teaspoon mustard seeds
- ½ teaspoon asafoetida
- ½ teaspoon white sesame seeds

- Mix together the dhokla flour and water as required, to make a thick batter. Add the ginger-chilli paste (optional), and salt, and ensure that the batter in smooth. Add the fruit salt, just before pouring the batter into the dhokla thali.
- Steam in a dhokla maker and remove once ready.
- For the tempering, heat the oil, add the mustard seeds, asafoetida and white sesame seeds.
- Pour the tempering over the dhokla uniformly. Garnish with coriander leaves and coconut. Cut into pieces and serve hot.

Note: *These dhoklas are yellow in colour.*

Safed Dhokla

- ¼ kg ready-made dhokla flour
- Water, as required
- 1 teaspoon coarse ginger-green chilli paste (optional)
- Salt to taste
- 1 packet Eno fruit salt
- 1 teaspoon red chilli powder

- Mix together the dhokla flour and water, as required, to make a thick batter.
- Add the ginger-chilli paste (optional), and salt, and ensure that the batter in smooth. Add the fruit salt just before pouring the batter into the dhokla thali.
- Steam it in a dhokla maker and remove once ready.
- Sprinkle the chilli powder over it and cut into pieces. Serve hot.

Note: *These dhoklas are white in colour.*

Panch Bheli Missal

- 1 vati each of sprouted green gram (moong), sprouted moth beans (matki), sprouted green peas (vatana), sprouted light vatana (harbhara)
- Water, as required
- Salt to taste
- ¼ teaspoon turmeric powder
- 2-3 crushed garlic cloves
- ½ vati fresh coconut
- 2-3 green chillies, finely chopped
- ½ inch ginger
- ¼ teaspoon cumin seeds
- ½ teaspoon jaggery
- 1 tomato or 1 teaspoon tamarind pulp
- Finely chopped onion, as required
- Finely chopped tomato, as required
- Coriander leaves, as required
- Pinch of chaat masala
- Fine sev, as required

Boil the sprouts with salt, turmeric powder and crushed garlic (optional).

Grind together the coconut, chillies, ginger and cumin seeds.

To the boiled sprouts, add the ground masala, jaggery and tamarind pulp and simmer for 2-3 minutes on low heat, till done.

Sprinkle the onions, tomatoes, coriander leaves, chaat masala and fine sev and serve hot.

Flower-Matar chi Karanji

- 1 vati greated cauliflower (phulkobi)
- 1 vati fresh green peas (vatana/matar)
- ½ teaspoon green chilli-ginger coarse paste
- 1 teaspoon turmeric powder
- ½ teaspoon red chilli powder
- 2 teaspoons lemon juice
- Salt to taste
- ½ teaspoon sugar
- ½ vati fine semolina
- Water, as required
- 1 vati refined flour
- Oil for deep-frying

For the tempering

- 1 teaspoon oil
- ½ teaspoon mustard seeds
- ½ teaspoon asafoetida
- ½ teaspoon carom seeds

- Coarsely grind the cauliflower and green peas.
- For the tempering, heat the oil, add the mustard seeds, asafoetida, turmeric powder and carom seeds.
- Add the chilli-ginger paste and add the cauliflower-green peas paste and mix well.
- Add the turmeric powder, chilli powder, lemon juice, salt and sugar. Mix well and cook covered for 2-3 minutes.
- Remove the lid and sauté till the mixture becomes dry. This is the stuffing for the karanji.
- Soak the semolina in 1-2 teaspoons of water. Add the refined flour, soaked semolina, salt, water and oil as required. Knead well to form a firm dough and set aside for an hour.
- To make the karanji, shape the dough into balls. Roll out the dough balls into puris.
- Place a spoonful of the stuffing on one half of the puri, fold the other half over it and seal the edges tightly.
- Heat the oil and deep-fry.
- Serve hot.

Kaakadiche Sandana

- 2 vatis rice (tandul)
- 1 cucumber (kaakadi)
- 2 teaspoons ghee
- 1½ teaspoons grated fresh coconut
- 1½ vatis jaggery
- 10 black cardamoms, peeled and crushed
- Ghee, for greasing
- ¼ vati finely chopped dry fruits

Wash, dry and grind the rice to make a fine flour.

Deseed and grate the cucumber.

Heat the ghee, add the cucumber, coconut, jaggery, cardamoms and rice flour. Stir well till the mixture thickens.

Grease a flat bottom cake mould with ghee, if required. Add the mixture to the mould and steam it in a pressure cooker without the whistle. Once done, remove from the mould and allow it to cool.

Garnish with chopped dry fruits, cut into pieces and serve.

Ravaa Cake

- 1 vati semolina (ravaa)
- 1 vati sour yoghurt (dahi)
- 1 vati milk
- 1 vati sugar
- 1 teaspoon baking soda
- ½ vati finely chopped dry fruits
- Ghee, for greasing

Mix together all the ingredients to make a smooth batter.

Grease a cake tin with ghee and pour the batter into it. Place the mould on a hot tawa. Cook covered on low heat, till done.

You can also prepare this cake by baking it in the microwave for 15-20 minutes.

Put a toothpick through it and if it comes out clean then the cake is ready.

Remove from the mould, and allow it to cool. Cut into pieces and serve.

Laal Bhoplyache Gharge

- ½ kg red pumpkin (laal bhopala)
- ½ kg jaggery
- Wholewheat flour, as required
- 2 teaspoons rice flour
- Oil for deep-frying + as required

- Chop the pumpkin into pieces.
- Add the jaggery to the pumpkin and mix well. Simmer on low heat till the jaggery melts and the mixture thickens. Allow it to cool.
- Add the wholewheat flour, rice flour and oil as required and knead to make a soft dough. Cover for 30 minutes.
- Shape the dough into balls and roll them out into puris. Heat the oil and deep-fry the puris. Serve hot with ghee.

Batatayachaa Kees

- 2 potatoes, grated thick
- 2 teaspoons ghee
- ½ teaspoon cumin seeds
- 1 green chilli, slit
- Salt to taste
- Pinch of sugar
- 2 tablespoons coriander leaves

- Place the grated potatoes in water or they will turn black quickly.
- Heat the ghee, add the cumin seeds and chilli.
- Add the strained grated potatoes and cook covered for 2-4 minutes on low heat, till done.
- Garnish it with coriander leaves.

Tip: *The potato can be replaced with sweet potato.*

Laadoo and Vadyaa

These sweets were always a staple in our school tiffins. A tasty snack for the hunger that strikes in between meals. These satisfy your cravings and are healthy too, as they are made from unprocessed home ingredients and do not contain any preservatives.

Policha Laadoo

- 2 vatis finely ground stale chappatis
- 1 vati hot ghee
- ½ vati jaggery
- ¼ vati powdered sugar

- Mix together all the ingredients and mould into laadoos.

Tilaache Laadoo

Variation 1

- ½ vati groundnuts
- ½ vati cashew nuts
- ½ vati roasted split Bengal gram (daale)
- ¼ kg unpolished sesame seeds (til)
- 2 tablespoons ghee
- ½ kg chikki jaggery (chikki gul)
- 1 teaspoon nutmeg powder
- 2 teaspoon sugar
- ½ vati finely grated dry coconut

- Coarsely grind the groundnuts, cashew nuts, and roasted split Bengal gram, separately.
- Dry-roast the sesame seeds for 5-7 minutes on a low heat. Add the ghee, jaggery, nutmeg powder and sugar, and stir till it the jaggery melts.
- Add the sesame seeds, coconut and all the coarsely ground nuts and mix well, take off the heat and immediately start shaping the mixture into laadoos.

Tip: *The laadoos have to be made when the mixture is hot as once the mixture cools it becomes hard, in which case heat it again on low heat.*

Tilaache Laadoo

Variation 2

- ¼ kg unpolished sesame seeds (til)
- ½ vati coarsely pounded groundnuts
- ½ vati roasted split Bengal gram (daale)
- ½ vati grated dry coconut
- 200 grams jaggery
- 1 teaspoon nutmeg powder
- 2 teaspoons ghee

Dry-roast the sesame seeds on low heat for 5-7 minutes. Allow them to cool.

Grind all the other ingredients along with the sesame seeds.

Shape this soft mixture into laadoos.

Aalivaache Laadoo

- ½ vati garden cress seeds (aaliva seeds)
- 1 vati milk
- 1 teaspoon ghee
- 1 vati grated fresh coconut
- ½ vati shredded jaggery
- ¼ vati almond, coarsely powdered
- 1 teaspoon nutmeg powder

Clean and soak the watercress in the milk for an hour.

Heat the ghee and add the watercress, fresh coconut, jaggery and cook on low heat for 5-7 minutes.

Transfer to a plate, add the rest of the ingredients. Mix well and take of the heat.

Grease your palms with ghee and shape the mixture into laadoos.

Methicha Laadoo

- 4 teaspoons fenugreek seeds (methi seeds)
- ½ kg dried dates (khaarik)
- ¼ kg dry coconut
- 200 gm dink
- 2 teaspoons ghee
- 1 nutmeg, powdered
- 50 grams poppy seeds
- ¼ kg dates, finely chopped
- ½ teaspoon garden cress seeds (aaliva seeds)
- 1 vati jaggery
- 1 vati sugar
- 15-20 almonds, powdered coarsely

- Dry-roast the fenugreek seeds and grind to a powder. Deseed the dried dates and pound them coarsely.
- Dry-roast the coconut and grind to a powder. Sauté the dink in ghee and then crush it into a powder.
- Mix together the fenugreek powder, nutmeg powder, poppy seeds almond powder and dates.
- Mix all the ingredients together except the jaggery and sugar.
- Heat a thick-bottomed pan and add the jaggery, sugar and enough water to immerse the sugar. Simmer on low heat for 5-7 minutes, till the jaggery and sugar forms a single thread consistency syrup.
- Add the syrup to the dry ingredients mixture and take of the heat.
- Grease your palms with ghee and shape the mixture into laadoos.

Dink Laadoo

- ½ kg sugared dried dates (khaarik)
- ¼ kg dry coconut
- 15-20 powdered almonds
- 1 teaspoon ghee
- 200 grams dink
- 1 nutmeg, powdered
- 1 vati jaggery
- 1 vati sugar
- 50 grams poppy seeds
- ½ vati oil

Deseed the dried dates and powder it coarsely. Grind the dry coconut to a fine powder. Grind the almond to a powder.

Heat the ghee and sauté the dink. Allow it to cool and then crush it. Add the nutmeg powder.

Heat the ghee, add the jaggery and sugar and stir well. Once it melts completely, add the rest of the ingredients and mix well and take of the heat.

Grease your palms with ghee and shape the mixture into laadoos.

Ravaa-Naaral Laadoo

- ½ vati ghee
- 1 vati semolina (laadoo ravaa)
- 1 vati grated fresh coconut (naaral)
- ½ vati sugar
- Water, as required
- 2 teaspoons cardamom powder
- ¼ vati milk

Tip: *Laadoo ravaa, which is finer than normal ravaa (semolina), is specially used for laadoos.*

Heat the ghee and sauté the semolina till fragrant.

Add the fresh coconut and sauté. Heat the sugar and add adequate water to immerse the sugar completely. Simmer on low heat till the sugar dissolves to form a single thread consistency syrup.

Add the semolina-coconut mixture, cardamom powder, and mix it well. If required, to moisten the mixture sprinkle some milk over it. Take off the heat.

Grease your palms with ghee and shape the mixture into laadoos.

Ravaa-Naaral Khavaa Laadoo

- 1 vati semolina (laadoo ravaa)
- 1 vati grated fresh coconut (naaral)
- 50 grams khavaa (khoya)
- 1 vati powdered sugar
- 1 teaspoon cardamom powder
- ¼ vati raisins and almond slices, together or used individually

- In a pressure cooker, add the semolina, coconut and khavaa in three separate containers and pressure cook till 3 whistles are released. Do not add water to any of it. Remove from the cooker once done.
- Sauté the semolina on low heat for 5 minutes. Allow all the ingredients to cool. Add the powdered sugar and cardamom powder. Mix together all the ingredients. Take off the heat.
- Grease your palms with ghee and shape the mixture into laadoos. Garnish with raisins or almond slices.

Ravaa–Besan Laadoo

- ¾ vati ghee
- 1 vati gram flour (besan)
- 1 vati semolina (laadoo ravaa)
- 1 vati powdered sugar
- 1½ vatis water
- 1 teaspoon cardamom powder
- 15-20 raisins

- Heat the ghee and sauté the gram flour and add the laadoo semolina to it, and continue to sauté till fragrant.
- Heat the sugar and add adequate water to immerse the sugar completely. Simmer on low heat till the sugar dissolves to form a single thread consistency syrup.
- Add the gram flour-semolina mixture to the syrup, mix well. Take off the heat. Grease your palms with ghee and shape the mixture into laadoos. Stick the raisins on top of each laadoo.

Besan Laadoo

1 vati ghee

2 vatis gram flour (besan)

Milk, as required

2 vatis powdered sugar

1 teaspoon cardamom powder

10-12 raisins

¼ vati dry fruit powder (optional)

Heat the ghee, add the gram flour and sauté for 5-8 minutes on low heat till fragrant. Sprinkle a little milk over it and keep it covered.

Once cool, add the powdered sugar, cardamom powder and raisins. Dry fruit powder can also be added. Mix well.

Grease your palms with ghee and shape the mixture into laadoos.

Gulpapdi Vadi

¾ vati ghee

1 vati wholewheat flour (kanik)

1 teaspoon cardamom powder or nutmeg powder

1 vati jaggery (gul)

Set aside 1 teaspoon ghee. Heat the remaining ghee and sauté the wholewheat flour on low heat for 5-6 minutes.

Allow it to cool and add the cardamom powder.

Add the reserved ghee to the jaggery and mix well.

Transfer to a heated pan and stir well till the jaggery melts.

Add the flour mixture to this, mix well and pour this mixture in a plate greased with ghee and spread it evenly.

Cool and cut into pieces and serve.

Khobrayaachi Vadi

- 1 teaspoon ghee
- 2-3 vatis grated fresh coconut (naaral/khobra)
- 1 vati fresh cream (taken from milk at home)
- 1 vati milk
- 4 vatis sugar
- 1 teaspoon cardamom powder

- Heat the ghee and add the coconut, cream, milk and sugar. Sauté continuously on low heat.
- As the sugar caramelises, the mixture starts to thicken and leave the sides of the pan.
- Pour this mixture on to a greased plate and allow it to cool. Cut the vadi and store or serve.

Tip: *We can add ½ vati of any of the following, to this recipe, to enhance the flavour and colour of the vadis: beetroot, carrot, boiled potato, tomato, mango, and bottle gourd.*

Aalyaachi Vadi

- ¼ kg ginger (aala)
- 10-15 almonds
- ¼ vati poppy seeds
- 1 vati milk
- 2 teaspoons sugar
- 1 teaspoon ghee
- 1 vati fresh cream (taken from milk at home)
- 1 teaspoon nutmeg powder

- Clean and peel the ginger and cut into small pieces. Soak the almonds and poppy seeds separately in warm water.
- Grind the ginger and poppy seeds separately. Grind the almond with milk. Mix these two pastes together. Add the sugar and nutmeg powder to the mixture.
- Heat the ghee and add the paste, some milk if required, fresh cream and stir continuously on low heat, till the mixture dries up. Spread it evenly on a greased plate and once cooled cut into pieces.

Tip: *This is a winter recipe.*

Tilaachi Vadi

- 1 vati sesame seeds (til)
- ¼ vati dry coconut, finely powdered
- 1 teaspoon ghee
- ½ vati shredded jaggery
- ½ vati coarsely pounded groundnuts
- ½ teaspoon cardamom powder

Dry-roast the sesame seeds and dry coconut, and grind to a powder.

Heat the ghee and add the jaggery, stir well.

Once the jaggery melts, add the pounded groundnuts and cardamom powder, and mix well.

Spread it evenly on a plate greased with ghee and allow it to cool.

Cut into pieces and serve.

Some useful tips

- Always plan your menu beforehand. That way the preparation will be easy and enjoyable.
- Whenever possible, try making dry masalas at home, as these are fresh and will enhance the flavour of the recipe.
- Always pre-roast groundnuts, peanuts, sesame seeds, ravaa and grated dry coconut. Store them in a tight lid jar, so they are handy while cooking.
- Soak the pulses for the usali and aamtis beforehand. They will get enough time to sprout and this makes them more nutritious.
- Always wash, de-thread and clean the vegetables before cooking.
- Soak all your leafy vegetables in water for at least 5 minutes so that any mud present in them, settles down. Then wash the vegetables under running water.
- Always wash, clean and pre-soak all dals and rice at least half an hour before you start cooking.
- While making sugar syrup, it is better to use a non-stick pan rather than a stainless steel pan.
- Whenever laadoos are made, first allow the mixture to cool completely, before moulding them and remember to always grease your palms with ghee.
- Remember, the key to a successful recipe is to always put in your heart and soul, while cooking.

Quantity conversion

1 vati = 150 grams or 4 ounces or ½ cup

Glossary

English	Marathi
Amaranth grains	Rajgirha
Amaranth leaves	Maath
Asafoetida	I ling
Baby potato	Goti batata
Banana	Kelaa
Banana flower	Kelphool
Bay leaves	Tamaalpatra
Bengal currant	Karvanda
Bitter gourd	Kaarli
Black cumin seeds	Shahjeera
Black peas	Kaala vatana
Black peppercorns	Kali miri
Black sesame seeds	Kale til
Bottle gourd	Dudhi bhopala/ dudhi
Brinjal	Vanga
Broken wheat	daliya
Buttermilk	Taak
Cabbage	Kobi
Carom seeds	Ova
Carrot	Gaajar
Cashew nuts	Kaju
Cauliflower	Phulkobi/ flower
Cauliflower	Phulkobi
Chilli	Mirchi
Cinnamon	Dalchini
Cloves	Lavang
Cluster beans	Gavaar
Coarsely ground samo seeds	Vari ravaa

English	Marathi
Coarsely grounded rice	Tandul ravaa
coarsely pounded groundnuts	Dana kut
coarsely pounded sesame seeds	Til kut
Coconut	Naaral
Colocasia	Alu
Coriander leaves	Kothimbir
Coriander seeds	Dhane
Cucumber	Kaakadi
Cumin seeds	Jeera
Curry leaves	Kadi patta
Dill	Shepu
Dolichos beans	Ghevda
Dried dates	Khaarik
Dried ginger	soonth
Drumstick sheng	Shevgaa
Dry ginger powder	Soonth
Fennel seeds	Badishep
Fenugreek leaves	Methi
Fenugreek seeds	Methi dane
Flat green beans shenga	Valachya
Flattened rice	Pohe
French beans	Farasbeech
Fresh field beans beans	Fresh field
Garbanzo beans	Harbhara
Garlic	Lasun
Ginger	Alaa
Gram flour	Besan

English	Marathi
Green chilli	Hirvi mirchi
Green peas	Vatana/ Matar
Green tomato	Kaccha tomato
Groundnuts	Shengdane
Guava	Peru
Horse gram	Kulith
Indian gooseberry	Avla
Ivy gourd	Tondli
Jackfruit	Phanas
Jackfruit seeds	Aathale
Jaggery	Gul
Kohlrabi	Navalkol
Kokum rinds	Amsool
Ladies' fingers	Bhendi
Lichen	Dagad phool
Lime	Limbu
Mint	Pudina
Mustard seeds	Mohori
Nigella seeds	Kalonji
Nutmeg	Jaiphal
Onion	Kanda
Pearl millet	Bajri
Pickle	Loncha
Pointed gourd	Parvar
Poppy seeds	Khas khas
Potato	Batata
Powdered sugar Saakhar	Pithi
Radish	Mula
Raw mango	Kairi
Red pumpkin	Laal bhopala
Refined flour	Maida
Rice	Tandul
Ridge gourd	Shirali
Roasted split Bengal gram	Daale
Safflower leaves	Kardai
Saffron	Kesar
Sago	Sabudana
Salt	Meeth
Samo seeds	Vari tandul
Semolina	Ravaa
Sesame seeds	Til
Skinless split black gram	Udid dal
skinless split green gram	Moong dal
Skinless split mustard seeds	Mohrichi dal
Small brinjal with a thorny stem	Kaateri vangi
Snake gourd	Padwal
Sorghum	Jowar
Spinach	Palak
Split Bengal gram	Chana dal
Split field beans	Val dal
Split red lentils	Masoor dal
Star anise	Chakriphool
Sugar	Saakhar
Sugar	Saakhar
Tamarind	Chinch
taro root	Alkudi/arbi
Turmeric	Halad
vermicelli	Shevyaa
Wheat grains	Gehu
White elephant foot yam	Suran
White sesame seeds	Safed til
Wholewheat flour	Kanik
Wood apple	Kavath
Yoghurt	Dahi